EVOLVING ECONOMICS

EVOLVING ECONOMICS

*Exploring the crises of capitalism
and a long-term vision of the economy
of a more sustainable, egalitarian, and
libertarian civilization*

Joseph P. Firmage

To order additional copies of this book, contact:
Xlibris Corporation
1-888-795-4274
www.Xlibris.com
Orders@Xlibris.com
99078

Dedicated to the children of earth

Introduction: Living Through a Singularity

"No complaint . . . is more common than that of a scarcity of money." [1]
—Adam Smith

In the United States of America in 2010, it's hard to turn on the television or open a magazine or newspaper and not be reminded of the omnipresence of economics in the minds of people. Of course, human preoccupation with money and other forms of capital isn't a new phenomenon. More than two centuries after they were written, Adam Smith's words still ring in our ears. And for as long as history has been recorded, our means of exchanging the goods and services springing from our Nature have been essential to our ability to sustain happy, productive lives. Our pocketbooks have been centers of attention ever since they were animal skin sacks filled with interesting trinkets worthy of exchange among hunting and gathering tribes. Notions of prosperity no doubt reach earlier still . . . for many millions of years we animals have found appreciation in the leaves of our nests.

Fortunate son that I was, the first time I recall coming face to face with a serious scarcity of money was around age 10 when I fell in love with astronomy, and wanted desperately to purchase a telescope. Being raised in a family of middle-class wealth—father a talented professor of constitutional law at the University of Utah, and mother a devoted homemaker taking great care of seven children—I was much better off than most young folks of my era. So I had a weekly allowance of a few dollars. But a few dollars per week would not any year soon purchase the telescope I sought, for this was not just any scope, but a really fine instrument—one suited for observation beyond Earth's moon and the planets circling our Sun, one suited for observation and photography of distant nebulae, star clusters, and galaxies as well. I found that my skill in caring for landscapes supplied just the demand necessary to motivate our neighbors to part with enough cash—with a lot of help from dad and mom—to buy that remarkable Schmidt-Cassegrain optical system. I learned early the economic rewards of yard work.

In subsequent years, a focus on computer science and much good fortune enabled me to become a self-made millionaire at age 23. I earned a seat at the table during commercial incubation of computer networking technologies. Since 1995, I have helped to raise several hundred million dollars for various information technology enterprises. I had the opportunity to be one of the many pioneers in the commercial adoption of the Internet, having been co-founder and CEO of USWeb, having there helped to serve a substantial percentage of Fortune 100 enterprises, presiding over dozens of mergers and acquisitions and taking our young company public. When I left the helm of the company in 1998, USWeb was a well-regarded multinational enterprise employing thousands of talented people across two continents. During my tenure, the company met or exceeded quarterly projections of Wall Street analysts. Though I made mistakes along the way, I was quite effective as a corporate executive, witness to workings of capitalism from inside and outside its inner sanctum.

From such a perspective within an engine room of economics, the scale of the early 21st century economy is breathtaking to behold—$40+ trillion in gross financial value of products and services emerging annually from millions of corporations touching every community of life on our planet.

This system is an integrating infrastructure through which billions of people are nourished, sheltered, healed, educated, engaged in productive lives, and honored as having intrinsic rights defined by constitutions and protected by systems of laws. Our economy gives us freedom to trade knowledge, tools, skills, services, and experiences. We enjoy common currencies of exchange for values across both generalizations and specializations. We have freedom to choose professions accessible to our internally-determined abilities, even though presently our choices are most often constrained by our externally-determined classes of wealth. Our economy gives us freedom to form enterprises that interact within a democratically-governable system. It fosters emergence of distributed organizations accountable to and protected by laws, organizations that can compete with one another as we stretch our ingenuities and diligence to reach ever-evolving objectives. Our economy sustains individual and organizational motivations seeking efficiencies and differentiations, continuously striving for the frictionless functioning and scale of service required by our planet's population of human beings.

In these respects, Adam Smith would be proud, and justifiably so. Billions of people are able to contribute to and receive value from a shared system in which collective productivity can supply individual demand, and individual productivity can supply collective demand. For those willing and equipped to play and win by its rules, this system offers a chance for people to lead happy and fulfilled lives.

To sustain such immense scale and complexity, economic machineries far beyond pocketbooks and bank accounts have evolved in the past century. Massive transaction webs interconnect enterprises across every industry; intricate financial services networks serve interests of wealth management; multilayered securities infrastructures and markets enable attribution of equity in anything real or virtual deemed of value, all supported by ever-more-elaborate legal code governing interactions among components in the system. Punctuated in the past three decades, logistics and information technologies cultivated by science have ripped away innumerable frictions from the gears of economic functioning, enabling the integration, scale and speed of global productivity and trade to rise to almost incomprehensible levels. And the same technologies transforming the value networks of multinational giants are now bringing to every desktop computer, family room TV, and corporate automaton an information dashboard which only ten years ago would have been the envy of the president of a nation, world economist or multinational CEO. For those few of us humans wealthy enough to employ modern information technology, our individual economic lives can be administered within an increasingly integrated global economic system, whose dashboard is as available as AOL on the latest wireless PC.

With modern technology, the world's economies have been developing year by year into an increasingly powerful, electronically integrated global mechanism, programmed with code evolving through the convergence of international economic and political paradigms.

In the face of systems of nearly unimaginable vitality, consequence and complexity, many people today believe that arguing for a large-scale evolution of economics is a somewhat anachronistic debate, a hopeless cause, or is simply off base. After all, isn't capitalism simply the best kind of economic paradigm that Nature can afford? Weren't the major philosophical questions about economics settled in the wars of the 20th century between capitalist and communist nations, with socialist paradigms still caught somewhere in a continuing identity crisis? Besides, with revolutions occurring in every field of science and technology simultaneously, it seems that, frightening recessions aside, capitalism is fostering a golden age of discovery and development, so why worry?

Aging economic-political-technological ecosystems are sustaining grave imbalances among the lives and liberties of human beings and in the systems of Nature. In 2010, the capitalist's notion of "a good life" is replete with fundamental contradictions, which are becoming increasingly visible for all the world's citizens to see.

Irreplaceable organs within Earth's tree of life are decaying and disappearing from overconsumption, and Nature is threatening to change the rules, by altering every ecosystem and life form through shifting weather patterns, disease and decay. Gaps between rich and poor are not closing. Society has no clear plan to serve an aging population needing a sustainable retirement. Ideological conflicts continue to simmer, while prices of weapons of mass destruction are falling into lower-class income brackets—an airplane loaded with fuel or anthrax, a suitcase-sized electromagnetic or nuclear weapon, or simply a phial of the latest variant of mad cow disease. Every kind of corporate and technological machine is growing exponentially more intelligent and powerful, as can be seen in a plot of the number of bits being processed and stored by computers. Human beings feel less fulfillment and increasing stress from work. The relative fall of religious dogmas has opened people to vital new freedoms while also inadvertently diminishing their faith in intrinsic values. New kinds and degrees of emotions, activities, chronic dysfunctions, cures and drug uses are appearing. Media can often appear schizophrenic, in streaming intellectually-uncontextualized, emotionally-charged experiences 24x7. (Consider a typical slice of prime-time TV: a woman runs through a lush, utopian meadow celebrating her new confidence in an allergy drug, followed by the Jaguar commercial all but showing the amazing sex you'll get if you buy or lease Ford's latest convertible, followed by the DiTech admonitions to consolidate your debt through a second mortgage on your home, and then on to Buffy, the Vampire Slayer. Now imagine yourself without the education you have; what are the effects of this series of impressions?)

It's clear that we are living during an era of unparalleled convergence among utopian and destructive trends. When the future consequences of both good and bad trends are overlaid upon a chart of time, the resultant figure has some resemblance to a form known in physics as a "singularity"—a point of such rapid, comprehensive and forceful change that the consequences are far too nonlinear to predict. If this concept proves a fair representation of current trends and their future interaction, then the generations of people alive today have been assigned by Nature a most challenging task: inventing and then performing aikido motions that will transform the momentum of the 20th century singularity into a stable 21st century foundation for a healthy and happy family of life on Earth.

As of this writing, I have no academic credentials in economics, so my words should be received with that fact in mind. But I do have a great deal of operational experience in business. Resulting from the time I have had to reflect upon issues observed while inside engine rooms of economics, I believe that there are lethal defects in our global economy that can only be corrected at a systemic level. A semi-conscious, instinctive realization of amorality, destructive greeds and pointless excesses produced by capitalism, along with insights into other fundamental issues of our time, drove me to resign from the helm of USWeb in late 1998. I decided to distance myself from capitalism, and have since interacted with it more tentatively, because of a belief that major changes to our economic paradigm are necessary if business is to come into alignment with the ethical compass required by humanity's future.

While the challenges we face seem to be disconnected crises, a common thread runs through them having everything to do with our economic paradigm. We have inherited a kind of economic matrix, which we use to serve each other in countless different ways. It is a heavy burden and a complex endeavor for all of us to consciously evolve the design and infrastructure of this matrix in such a way that it is able to sustain perpetually the kind of civilization worthy of humanity's multi-billion year Cosmic history and destiny. Within this challenge also can be seen a profound opportunity for the compassionate renewal of human culture and community, and of Nature as an organic whole.

Recognizing the vital strengths of capitalism, I am more convinced today than ever that we must transform our world economic system if human beings are to survive and thrive upon a blue-green Cosmic coral reef rich in the kind of life no money can purchase.

Part I
A View of the System and State of Our Economy

Part I of Evolving Economics assesses the architecture and
state of the capitalist economic system at the turn of the millennium.
It is argued that, while capitalism has succeeded in enhancing social
well-being and freedom by replacing autocratic human governance of
economic activity with objective rules of trade, capitalism has
established its own formal, autocratic central plan: financial and
legal code motivating perpetual growth in revenue and profit flows to
private self-interests. Endemic social dysfunctions attributable to
defects in this architecture are explored in broad but
fundamental terms. Scenarios of the future are sketched,
indexed to the evolution of our economic paradigm.

Chapter 1
Concerns of Measures and Balances

*"Such is the delicacy of man alone, that no object is produced to his
liking. He finds that in everything there is need for improvement . . . .
The whole industry of human life is employed not in procuring the
supply of our three humble necessities, food, clothes and lodging, but in
procuring the conveniences of it according to the nicety and
delicacy of our tastes."[2]*

—Adam Smith

Questions about capitalism might begin with Adam Smith's faith in the quest for opulence. Centuries ago, with great wisdom and foresight for his time, he said, "Little else is requisite to carry a state to the highest degree of opulence from the lowest barbarism but peace, easy taxes, and a tolerable administration of justice: all the rest being brought about by the natural course of things."[3] It's hard to disagree with those words. Indeed, it is entirely clear why an economic paradigm whose invisible hand is programmed ever to expand the opulence of materiality would inspire the imagination of intensely conscious animals such as 18th century human beings. We were living painfully short lives, inhabiting austere dwellings, subject to every whim of a deeply-mysterious Nature, in need of objective collective organizing principles and ways to distribute resources in some proportion to contribution, lacking universal methods of exchange for our talents, yet powerfully drawn to the seductive allure of opulence displayed by the affluent.

But centuries later, it is equally clear that Earth cannot support forms of opulence as wasteful as those yielded by the invisible hand of 20th century capitalism.

My first and deepest concern about capitalism is the root motive yielding perpetual growth of opulence. It is a defect in the logic of capitalism contributing to every other economic dysfunction that I will review in this essay. I am deeply troubled by the manner in which capitalism measures success: many of the most basic and universal metrics within capitalism employ 'dumb sums' that ignore relative and contextual factors. I call these measures dimensionally-deficient metrics—measurement systems lacking or hiding information sufficient to enable the evaluation of yielded indices in context of reality. In physics terms, they are scalar and vector sums conveying no information but size and growth.

Some of capitalism's most basic dimensionally-deficient measures are the meters of success used almost every day by millions of business executives around the world:

- *Revenue*, reflecting natural or artificial demand, as the magnitude of incoming currency flow, of which . . .
- *Profit* is the part of incoming currency flow achieved through arbitrage of value (the process of "buying low and selling high"); and . . .
- *Growth*, measured as the increase of revenue and *profit*.

If capitalism is thought of as a computer program for the economy of human civilization (as it very well can and should be), these meters of success are part of its core program code: the logic followed by all capitalist entities. Because these measures are largely context-free quantities—absent intrinsic qualitative dimensions—notions of "more is better" and "less is crisis" govern their interpretation, particularly given the narrow interpretation of "self-interest" embedded in the logic of capitalism.

The goal of ever ascending material opulence translates in practice to the notion that more revenue, more profit, and more growth are always good. As measured by the code of profit and loss statements of today's capitalism, growth in demanded supply and private profit there from is held to be equally good regardless of whether it's serving real needs of people or the capital interests behind brand-created desires for branded "values".

And since corporations are defined with status of "persons" in capitalism's legal code, non-organic interests within the economic machine itself are also free to seek forms of self-aggrandizing opulence, behavior guided primarily by these self-measures.

Capitalism is thus presently not programmed to understand the potential value of lesser opulence, or different forms of opulence that reduce these flows of its currency. In other words, by virtue of the metrics in its code, *capitalism cannot understand the potential value of zero or negative growth in revenue or profit.* Zero or negative growth in the currency flow representing aggregate consumption causes capitalism to sink into recession or depression, and since human livelihoods are presently hitched to the logic of capitalism, society follows.

In this way, capitalism's architecture favors ever-larger flow structures in its contests—it seeks ever more opulence, precisely as it was designed to do. The metrics of the capitalist profit and loss statement appear to have no in-built mechanism to prevent them from rewarding cancerous kinds of growth. How is it possible for capitalism to do a good job intrinsically of balancing relative values of rights, purposes, sustainabilities or wastes in its processes, when it respects enterprise success measures little more evolved than *"how big is it, and how fast is it growing?"*

Many economists would argue that capitalism does possess a system to self-correct for destructive growth tendencies, namely consumer choice. While this is true in some circumstances, it is clearly specious in principle or in practice to shift the primary burden of limiting capitalist excesses onto the shoulders of consumers, whipped as we are into consumptive frenzy through corporate PR and advertising at every turn, forced as we are to put our shoulders to capitalism's wheels, frightened for our individual well-being should aggregate consumption begin to waver. We are ever-mandated by bosses, politicians, economists, and all other species of pundits to "sustain growth".

The utter impossibility and injustice of depending upon consumer choice to restrain capitalism's self-interest-driven excesses are particularly evident juxtaposed with two facts. First, capitalism is not intrinsically programmed to educate its consumers on truth. Since the economic physics driving long-term human well being is not, in fact, the force of "consumer choice", but rather "consumer choice x consumer education", consumer choice alone cannot be assumed to represent a proper guidance system for long-term decision-making. Consider the diamond trade. Buying a diamond—a shiny bit of carbon—may seem utterly harmless, until one recognizes the effect it is having on the developing populations and capital interests fighting over the resource. Yet empirically speaking, neither the diamond store nor CNN is likely to characterize your purchase as destructive.

Second, even if capitalism were to be reprogrammed to educate its consumers on truth (which it cannot do and remain viable in its present form), in many cases vital truths are not knowable. We are moving into an era in which the invisible hand of economics can wear the glove of every advanced technology known, even of life itself, creating complexity in aggregate future effects of individual producer-consumer actions impossible even for the entire scientific community to foresee. Nowhere is the risk of this situation clearer than in the question of genetic engineering by capitalist corporations. As chaos theorists might suggest, the flap of butterfly's wing—say, washing our dishes with antibiotic dish soap—can yield a hurricane—genetically strengthened super-germs—years later. The fact that we cannot accurately quantify a risk does not mitigate it.

The problem of deficient economic measures is not limited to profit and loss (P&L) statements of corporations. All kinds of fiscal constructs built upon defective metrics risk being operationally defective. Among the most obvious are measures of corporate equity value. Measures of revenue, profit, and growth thereof are the determinants of equity values, driving decisions of equity holders, who "own" corporate management. Equity markets thus increase the control of P&L measures with even less sensation of downstream consequences than the P&Ls to which they are indexed. A 50% rise or drop in the stock value of Archer Daniels Midland does not mean that the value to humanity of ADM's activity has risen or fallen by 50%, rather it means the perceived financial value of the paper or bits representing its opaquely-owned shares has changed. Which of the two value systems—human values or private equity values—drives the day-to-day decisions of ADM?

All forms of interest, equities and the growing variety of financial instruments defined by a real-time calculus, such as options, derivatives, and futures can magnify effects of dimensionally-defective metrics. Decisions of a securities holder can appear to have no unethical consequences, but often the inevitable Newtonian reactions are several years, several continents, several social classes, several species, or simply several brokers removed from the decision maker. In similar fashion, communities of economic decision makers forming all kinds of markets establish amoral venues for exchange, which can only equilibrate functions they sense (measure)—and so are only as good or bad as the effects of their code. They therefore also sustain and can magnify the effects of deficient economic measures.

Thus, it can be seen how information deficiency of capitalism's ticker-toy performance measures can allow disservice to be labeled as service, unhealthy products to be labeled as goods, obesity of consumption to be labeled as growth in output, and destruction of Nature to be labeled as profit.

I will stress that this concern—measures of success that depend upon blind revenue, profit and continuous growth benefiting private self-interests—is the primary defect I identify in capitalism. The defect is so fundamental to the foundations of our world economy in 2010 that it cannot be addressed without a significant evolution of the charters, laws and ethic of macroeconomic activity as a whole.

~

The lack of context in the dimensions of economic measures can yield other concerning effects—effects less obvious than the problem of uncontrollable growth, but resulting in no less of a predicament. Consider the consequences of the way capitalism measures "productivity" and "output". By virtue of dimension-deficiency and opacity in measurement, calculation, reporting and appraisal, capitalism is currently blind to whether "inputs" are provided by life or automation. If a machine can be developed which is capable of producing a given unit of output for less capital than is required to yield the same output through human labor, then human beings will at some point no longer be employable for that input-output function.

This problem—comprehension of and respect for the intrinsic rights and nature of "inputs"—has generated intense friction between labor and capital interests ever since the industrial revolution began. Now the issue is moving beyond muscles to brains: machines are increasingly capable of replacing human beings in roles of logistics, customer service, teaching, entertainment, decision support, research and analysis, and any kind of information processing. It takes less than 20 hours of human labor to assemble a modern automobile from pre-built components; soon it will take less than 10 hours. The rest of the hours—perhaps soon just minutes—come from robotics. What percentage of business telephone calls are answered by human beings today? What percentage of stock trading decisions are made by human beings versus computer algorithms today? For what percentage of the average day is the typical American child engaged and entertained by machines versus human beings? What percentage of human proteins will be mapped by human beings versus computers? What percentage of the circuitry of next generation microprocessors will be designed not by human beings, but by microprocessors?

Within the logic and structures of modern capitalism, a human being must invent or compete with accelerating computerized treadmills to earn a wage. This is a deep and fundamental problem, not because we employ technology to do the things it does, and not because of any evil somehow inherent in science or technology, but because of economic protocols which dividend the leverage (and therefore also guide the evolution) of science and technology to serve short-term capital interests in wealth concentration rather than long-term labor interests in liberty—time free of work for subsistence.

Marx and Lenin and many others since have examined aspects of this problem, but misprescribed and mis-applied communist and socialist paradigms are not the solutions.

Individual freedom of economic activity rightly prevailed over domination by state autocracy. But the capitalist ought not be overly boastful, for the full dimensions of the challenge to labor in balancing human interests with those of economically programmed machines would have been impossible to fully anticipate in the era of Adam Smith and other early founders of the philosophy of capitalism.

One of the primary reasons the U.S. economy has been so robust in recent decades is that its citizens have been fortunate enough to earn a living doing what machines haven't (yet) been able to do by themselves: inventing better machines. In part through the virtues of constitutional and economic commitments to and legal enforcement of human rights, responsibilities, and freedoms, the United States was the fertile soil for the emergence of high technology wonders. Through the leverage of assets and the tenacity of capitalism's intellectual property laws now becoming the rules of global trade, Western technological dominance has been maintained ever since. Centers of wealth and owners of intellectual property have fundamental advantages in perpetuating dominance in downstream innovation. Perhaps these reasons explain why Americans feel less instinctive anxiety about global capitalism than their international peers. Such confidence is not likely well-placed.

In the context of increasing populist anger against American capitalism, it should also be stressed that many supposedly non-capitalist nations employ the very same principles in their economies, often with less regard for principle. Even though such nations do not have the scale or sophistication of American markets or free-running corporate ecosystems, capitalism's fundamental self-interest-driven performance measures drive behavior nonetheless, in some cases with far worse consequences for their citizens. Given lower standards of respect for law, democratic representation, and basic fairness, privateinterest-driven economic activity becomes far more destructive—whether called capitalism or not. Corruption in developing nations dramatically magnifies effects of the defects in self-interest-driven economics. Populations in developing nations increasingly incensed at Western economic domination must also examine the governing ethics of their own regimes.

This particular flaw in capitalism's logic—the misplacement of accrued and continuing benefit from automation into the hands of capital versus labor—is practiced everywhere, and has created an unstable, top-heavy world economic order that will no doubt equilibrate, through enlightenment of leaders of governments, business and finance as they consciously evolve the world's economic paradigm to make temporary their status as a capitalist autocracy, or through devastating international revolutions by justifiably angry citizens who will make it so.

The epic challenge of our era as Human Beings of a beautifully organic Nature is to rebalance our rights with those of capital interests owning the ideomechonomics—economically programmed mechanisms—through which we serve each other. We must fundamentally evolve the code guiding capital interests and increasingly powerful machines, redefining the purposes for which they operate and grow, reframing the rights they will have with respect to Nature. I believe that instinctive public awareness of the depth of this challenge is evidenced by the spectrum of protest movements that stepped up confrontation with the globalization of neoliberal capitalism at the turn of the millennium.

~

Raising my concerns about capitalism's broken measures and imbalances to a higher perspective, I believe that dimensionally-deficient metrics of "success" such as "profit" result in equally deficient measures of "value" across the landscape of economic—and therefore social—activity.

Capitalism's notion of profit can be interpreted as a form of arbitrage—the process of buying at a lower price in one market and selling at a higher price in another market—self-interests pocketing the difference. Profit and arbitrage are not equivalent in the minds of most economists, and there are indeed distinctions between the two concepts in operation4. But by identifying one market as the source of inputs paid for by the corporation and the other market as the destination for outputs sold by the corporation, we can gain useful insights into the nature of currency flows through capitalist enterprises, and the notion of profit as arbitrage can be evaluated.

There are several kinds of arbitrage. For this discussion, let me represent the kind I am referring to as value arbitrage. Finance 101 teaches us that measures of after-tax profit (value arbitrage) from a corporation's operations are key determinants of the equity value of the enterprise. It is therefore easy to see that an entity whose operations cannot or choose not to produce value arbitrage—entities that cannot or choose not to sell their outputs at higher prices than the cost of their inputs—are considered by economics today formally to be valueless or worse. If a private capital interest does not profit from an entity's operations, regardless of the actual value of its productivities to people in general or Nature, the entity's operations are deemed by capitalism to have no equity value.

Simple questions succinctly reveal the defects of such a paradigm:

Q Is an intellectual property freely copied and used by millions of poor people really less "valuable" than if instead the same intellectual property is sold for a fee to thousands of rich people? Are qualitative perfections "valuable" only if they are arbitraged (bought low, sold high) by capitalism?

Q Is news "valuable" only if it generates an instantly-gratified audience? Is the public education process "valuable" only if it is more profitable than entertainment? Which is more "valuable" to report: starvation and death of millions in Africa or the latest sex "scandal" in politics? Which obtains more airtime today?

Q Is Philip Morris more or less "valuable" than the World Wildlife Fund? Capitalism says that the operations of the former are worth billions and those of the latter are worth nothing. Are specialized organizations "valuable" only if their productivities are arbitraged by capitalism?

Q Is energy "valuable" only if it doesn't flow freely? Are perfectible efficiencies "valuable" only if they are arbitraged by capitalism?

Q Are human beings "valuable" only if their output is more profitable than equivalent output from machines? Think about this seriously for a moment: are life forms "valuable" only if they are arbitraged (bought low, sold high) by capitalism?

Capitalism's measures of corporate and asset value index to time-depreciations of private profit from operations, and thus capitalism is myopic to values unsupportive of private arbitrage or the infrastructure enabling arbitrage—values such as meanings, rights, qualities, purposes, effects, and durabilities. Worse, capitalism is totally blind to the values of those assets that we cannot or choose not to arbitrage at all. If we cannot or choose not to allow private interests to sell certain outputs at greater prices than the costs of the inputs, those outputs are appraised by capitalism to be "unmonetizable". An untouched forest is "unmonetizable". A human being who cannot outcompete a machine is "unmonetizable". Nearly free, sustainable energy systems are "unmonetizable". A health regimen that does not require expensive intervention or drugs is "unmonetizable", apart from the business of selling books, videos and conferences on healthy living. Sharing critical inventions with developing populations is not "monetizable". Such things will not be supported by capitalism. If you can't buy it low and sell it high, private capital will not endeavor to support it. Thus can the goods of the many be outweighed by the greed of the ones.

Mainstream economists will argue that profit is the consequence of the laws of prices, whereby the subjective value perceived by each side of a transaction must be roughly equivalent, or no exchange will occur. While this is empirically true in practice today, it strikes me more as description of soft extortion than ethical economics. A third party observer of any such transaction, such as an insurer or a bank, typically has no problem in providing an objective description of the arbitrage. From this perspective, we are left with a rather stunning realization:

in a fundamental sense, the institutionalization of arbitrage as the primary performance metric of business means that society measures the success of an economic entity by the degree of asymmetry in its value exchanges. In other words, the capitalist notion of profit—the less labor-time (money) a seller has to give in comparison to the greater labor-time (money) the buyer gives in exchange, the more "successful" the seller is appraised. This could be described as the antithesis of compassion. The implications of this are hard to overstate.

We have begun to glimpse some of the unexpected consequences of the capitalist logic: the perpetual escalation of self-focused opulence—formally driven by measurement-enforced pursuit of growth of revenue and profit line items in the financial statements of capitalism's private interest "persons"—is perpetuating ancient and barbaric inequities, confounding peace among classes, sustaining high taxes paid to capitalist governors through excess consumption of their overbuilt branded values, withholding economic justice for generations of laborers everywhere, and placing at increasing risk the very survival of intelligent life on Earth.

Chapter 2
Concerns of Structures and Processes

"Imagine a wondrous new machine, strong and supple, a machine that reaps as it destroys. It is huge and mobile, something like the machines of modern agriculture but vastly more complicated and powerful. Think of this awesome machine running over open terrain and ignoring familiar boundaries. It plows across fields and fencerows with a fierce momentum that is exhilarating to behold and also frightening. As it goes, the machine throws off enormous mows of wealth and bounty while it leaves behind great furrows of wreckage."[5]

—William Greider

Built upon a matrix of dimensionally-deficient measures intrinsically unable to maintain proper balances, it should come as no surprise that resulting structures and processes of capitalism often can become grossly inequitable, perverse, ineffective or simply unstable.

Underlying its tendency towards inequity, capitalism attempts to cast the augmentation of wealth as a moral activity through its notion of how self-interests operate. The logic goes that if all capitalist entities just follow isolated self-interests bounded only by laws, it'll all just somehow work out in the end. One of the results in practice is this: an entity which takes wealth—a larger share of well-being pie—is honored and rewarded by capitalism more aggressively than an entity which increases the actual wealth of others—giving real well-being. So interest and profit—value arbitrages creating a net wealth flow back to wealth and the superior capitalist—are today just assumed always to be "good" and "right". Capitalist entities that demonstrate compassion—reducing their profits by giving to others more than rounding errors of net wealth flow—are penalized and dishonored.

Even if the operation of capitalism's self-interest logic were to be sustainable perpetually on the level of main street shops and family farms, as it might be under certain conditions of restraint, intelligence, and compassion, it is intellectually bankrupt to argue that capital self-interests of non-human corporate "persons" simultaneously operating will yield genuine long-term human interests, when such corporate entities are measured for success primarily in 20th century P&L terms—raw growth in flow of currency to their private, opaque interests—the more and faster the better.

Q   How motivated is the energy industry to discover and deploy means of electricity generation that would dramatically reduce per-capita energy spending?

Q   How motivated is the computer industry to create computer architectures that accommodate simple, near-perpetual upgrading of inexpensive internal components, rather than motivating complete unit replacement every 36 months?

Q   How motivated is the pharmaceutical industry to find cures or acknowledge alternative treatments for chronic maladies, if such cures or alternative practices would substantially reduce the currency flow from sales of symptom-focused drug or other technological regimens that are more chronically profitable?

Q   As but three of ubiquitous small examples relevant only in their aggregate effects, why on Earth need a package of 10 pieces of "new and improved" chewing gum be encased in individualized plastic and metal foil containers, costing consumers almost two dollars per pack? Why is a half-liter plastic bottle of water (no more pure than water from a tap) sold for two dollars per bottle? Why do automobile manufacturers seductively market SUVs to suburbanites who generally have no need for such wasteful contraptions? Are such universal consumer marketing ploys to be considered ethical because they enhance corporate profit margins?

Revealing the more subtle manner in which the invisible hand of economics also animates government, it is fair to ask how motivated financially the macro-consciousness of law enforcement is to enable a society whose need for law enforcement is dramatically reduced. Regarding how many other overweight government departments should the same question be asked? How much of humanity's inability to chain the dog of war springs from the flow of $1 trillion/year through the world's weapons makers, behavior enforced by equity owners and markets with no deeper instructions formally coded into their success formulae than "GROW!"?

Consider the words of United States Marine Corps Major General Smedley D. Butler, twice awarded the Medal of Honor (1914, 1917), taken from a speech given shockingly long ago, in 1931:

"A racket is best described, I believe, as something that is not what it seems to the majority of people. Only a small inside group knows what it is about. It is conducted for the benefit of the very few at the expense of the masses . . .

"The trouble with America is that when the dollar only earns 6 percent over here, then it gets restless and goes overseas to get 100 percent. Then the flag follows the dollar and the soldiers follow the flag.

"I wouldn't go to war again as I have done to protect some lousy investment of the bankers. There are only two things we should fight for. One is the defense of our homes and the other is the Bill of Rights. War for any other reason is simply a racket.

"There isn't a trick in the racketeering bag that the military gang is blind to. It has its 'finger men' to point out enemies, its 'muscle men' to destroy enemies, its 'brain men' to plan war preparations and a 'Big Boss', Super-Nationalistic-Capitalism . . .

"I spent thirty-three years and four months in active military service as a member of this country's most agile military force, the Marine Corps. I served in all commissioned ranks from Second Lietenant to Major General. And during that period, I spent most of my time being a high class muscle-man for Big Business, for Wall Street and for the Bankers. In short, I was a racketeer, a gangster for capitalism . . .

"I helped make Honduras 'right' for American fruit companies in 1903. I helped make Mexico, especially Tampico, safe for American oil interests in 1914. I helped make Haiti and Cuba a decent place for the National City Bank boys to collect revenues in. I helped in the raping of half a dozen Central American republics for the benefits of Wall Street. The record of racketeering is long. I helped purify Nicaragua for the international banking house of Brown Brothers in 1909-1912. I brought light to the Dominican Republic for American sugar interests in 1916. In China I helped to see to it that Standard Oil went its way unmolested.

"During those years, I had, as the boys in the back room would say, a swell racket. Looking back on it, I feel that I could have given Al Capone a few hints. The best he could do was to operate his racket in three districts. I operated on three continents."

Sharing tactics of value arbitrage and—as important—a presently-unavoidable need for job preservation, capitalist notions of self-interest operate in almost every financial transaction and major governing decision made at the beginning of the 21st century. As pointed out above, an action absent the prompt, measurable yield of private wealth augmentation or other self-focused interest, to say nothing of the opposite action of charity, is at best ignored or at worst hidden or destroyed as formally valueless by the immune system of capitalism.

The resulting ethical conflict is not broadly understood by ordinary people and is certainly not broadcast by capitalist media, so it tends to operate only at a sub-conscious level. The cumulative effects of this on all of us moral animals deserve serious study. I would speculate that this self-focused programmatic code within capitalism contributes to serious, infectious pains of aspirituality and depression felt by so many people today.

Wealth augmentation becomes most problematic when it is allowed to self-reinforce into accelerating wealth concentration, and this is accomplished through the leverage of capitalism's systems of private ownership of properties such as real estate and patents, and equities such as stocks. Assets are presumably defined by their collective recognition as economic values, measured by their ability to yield their owners continuing income and influence over underlying functions, which benefits can be turned around and reinvested in further benefit-generating properties. But where in the formal success metrics of corporations or equity markets can be found measurements which motivate egalitarian distribution of assets? Is this not a central reason why the gap between rich and poor remains an unsolvable crisis?

Quoting6 from the writings of Jeff Gates, a gifted and prolific analyst of modern economics:

"In the U.S., the bipartisan embrace of the current economic model (known as 'neoliberal economics') quickened the pace of redistribution from the bottom [of the economic ladder] to top over the past two decades. For example, the wealth of the Forbes 400 richest Americans grew an average $1.44 billion each from 1997-2000 for an average daily increase in wealth of $1,920,000 per person ($240,000 per hour or 46,602 times the minimum wage).

"From 1983-1997, only the top five percent of U.S. households saw an increase in their net worth, while wealth declined for everyone else. The share of the nation's after-tax income received by the top 1 percent nearly doubled from 1979-1997. By 1998, the top-earning 1 percent had as much combined income as the 100 million Americans with the lowest earnings. The top fifth of U.S. households now claim 49.2 percent of national income while the bottom fifth gets by on 3.6 percent. Between 1979 and 1997, the average income of the richest fifth jumped from nine times the income of the poorest fifth to roughly 15 times. The average hourly earnings for white-collar males was $19.24 in 1997, up from $19.18 in 1973. These results reflect the key distributional principle guiding our current economic model: 'Drink your fill and thirst for more.' This is the model we insist be emulated abroad.

"The premise of neoliberal-led globalization is that a rising tide lifts all boats—that the 80 percent of humanity living in developing countries will become better off, as will those 20 percent living in developed countries. The UN Development Program (UNDP) reports that 80 countries have per capita incomes lower than a decade ago. Sixty countries have grown steadily poorer since 1980. In 1960, the income gap between the fifth of the world's people living in the richest countries and the fifth in the poorest countries was 30 to 1. By 1990, the gap had widened to 60 to 1. By 1998, it had grown to 74 to 1. Meanwhile, the world's 200 wealthiest people doubled their net worth in the four years to 1999, to $1,000 billion. Three billion people live on $2 or less per day while 1.3 billion of those get by on less than $1 per day. With global population expanding 80 million each year, World Bank President James D. Wolfensohn cautions that, unless we address this 'challenge of inclusion,' 30 years hence we will have 5 billion people living on less than $2 per day.

"The UNDP reports that two billion people suffer from malnutrition, including 55 million in industrial countries. Current trends suggest that in three decades we could inhabit a world where 3.7 billion people suffer from malnutrition. UNDP's assessment: 'Development that perpetuates today's inequalities in neither sustainable nor worth sustaining.' Prosperity is not trickling down, it's gushing up. Yet this is the model we insist on spreading abroad.

"Today's capital market-led 'emerging markets' development model is poised to replicate U.S. wealth patterns worldwide. For instance, 61.7 percent of Indonesia's stock market value is held by that nation's 15 richest families. The comparable figure for the Philippines is 55.1 percent and 53.3 percent for Thailand. Worldwide, there's now roughly $60 trillion in securitized assets (stocks, bonds, etc.), with an estimated $90 trillion in additional assets that will become securitizable as the emerging markets model spreads. We may yet create a world where a handful of already well-to-do families worldwide pocket more than 50% of that $90 trillion in financial wealth. This is the model we insist on spreading worldwide.

"The industrial nations channel $326 billion a year in subsidies to their own farmers while (a) restricting agricultural imports from developing countries and (b) insisting that debtor nations repay their foreign loans in foreign currency, which they can earn only by exporting. According to a World Bank study, the elimination of import barriers against textiles, sugar and other key exports of developing nations would raise their export earnings by more than $100 billion a year—enough, if those restrictions had been removed since 1982, to repay all debts presently owed. In other words, the richest nations have insisted that poor nations pay debts but have refused the entry of goods offered in payment. In 1999, leaders of the G-7 industrial nations announced the debt initiative for Heavily Indebted Poor Countries (HIPCs), aiming to cap debt service for each of the world's 41 poorest country's at 15-20 percent of export earnings. By comparison, after World War I, the victors set the limit on German reparations at 13-15 percent of exports. Is that the standard against which modern-day democracy is to be measured?"

More than ample empirical data now exists to conclude that capitalism possesses insufficient intrinsic motivations to foster democratic fairness in ownership—beneficence and control—of societal assets. The core code of capitalistic function—P&Ls and balance sheets and all measures built thereupon—do not measure the equity of democratic distribution of such things. Hence, asset ownership continues to concentrate, in many ways that are not obvious but terribly insidious.

Q Are the communities of humans that were first to develop modern technology to remain forever rich at the expense of the other 90% of humanity, by passing from one private interest to another retained ownership of and self-sustaining advantage concerning natural resources and intellectual property, interests now able to operate worldwide through globalization and "development"?

Q   In the context of globalization of trade, how likely is it that local interests within a developing economy can compete effectively against staggeringly huge war chests of cash and decades of intellectual property inherited within developed economies? In this respect, what, in fact, is the liberation of trade enabling the momenta of capital interests to do?

Renowned New York Times foreign affairs columnist William Friedman—a cautious supporter of the globalization of capitalism—suggests, "If market forces get totally out of whack—if people feel that the system has become so crazy that the connection between hard work and a better standard of living gets severed and therefore no amount of painful reforms or belt-tightening will get them a share—then this system is in danger. But we have not yet reached that point—yet."[7]

His cautionary advice is useful for the under-read leaders of business and economics today. But he is gravely understating the seriousness of the situation. Among the uncountable consequences of the operation of capitalism through the past 500 years, one genocidal crime repeatedly stands out: developing nations are regularly cannibalized by their more 'developed' 'mentors'. We in the 'developed' world are drenched in the blood of entire societies.

~

The concern of unfairness in ownership and control of leverage-producing assets has taken on entirely new urgency in recent years, as science and engineering have clothed the invisible hand of economics with exponentially increasing physical powers. The leverage of technological assets (both "hard" and "soft" and now even "wet") today is focused on fulfilling short-term capital interests, which interests have status as "persons" in capitalism's code of law. With the intelligence and power of automation rising in many dimensions at once, wealthy individuals and corporate machines can scale the effects of their interests like never before. As explained above, the labor interest in freedom from labor is not programmed to be the primary result of automation, resulting in at least three ethical concerns that can be seen in increasingly clear relief.

The first is an unethical suppression of certain paths of technological innovation. The second is the opposite—an unethical chase of risky paths of innovation. The third is the utilization of advanced technology for manipulation of the economy itself.

To the first, massive capital interests are not motivated to make their owned industries so efficient as to dramatically reduce the currency flow of revenue (by large, unreplaced reductions in prices), nor so available as to reduce the currency flow of profit from scarcity, running through their corporations. So, with billions still in poverty and most of the rest of us working harder and harder to make ends meet, consider the following reality:

➢ Communications and computing industries have entered into a severe "overcapacity" condition, where supply is too cheap and ubiquitous, yet still too expensive for most of the world's population, to maintain preexisting revenue streams; corporations are cutting workforces and becoming increasingly automated, concentrating suppliers into cartels to prop up profits; we could make daily use of communications and computing nearly free in perhaps 15 years, but information technology giants are not motivated to do so;

➢ Energy generation industries have been controlling supply to prop up profits for decades; meanwhile, the price of subsistence-level energy consumption exceeds the earning power of much of the world's population; technologies are possible that could make daily use of energy nearly free within perhaps 20 years, yet they receive almost no R&D funding or have been suppressed;

➢ Transportation technologies are possible that could make daily travel nearly free within perhaps 50 years, yet they receive almost no R&D funding or have been suppressed;

➢ Building and architecture technologies are on the horizon that could make daily use of habitation structures nearly free in perhaps 100 years, yet they receive almost no R&D funding or have been suppressed.

In short, power centers of capitalism do not see the value in innovations so leveragable as to drop prices nearly to zero, since such prices would decimate revenue lines of P&Ls. Nor can capitalism see the value in supplies so abundant that supply limitation disappears altogether, since such abundance would take down profit lines of P&Ls. Hence, highly competitive markets for nearly infinitely leveragable and highly beneficial technologies, such as free communications, solar and wind power, rechargeable batteries, and advanced-physics energy and propulsion systems are ignored, shunned, or otherwise secreted away by the system. Their output is tougher to arbitrage and may make obsolete huge money flows along with the hierarchies feeding upon them.

This problem can be seen in yet clearer relief in the raging battles over intellectual property rights. By virtue of its ability to be copied at almost no physical cost, intellectual property is intrinsically an infinitely leveragable technology. Are we human beings not sufficiently inventive to discover an economic protocol that could fund creators of valued works of art and technology while enabling the open sharing of intellectual property? Why can't we figure out a way to share our science, songs, and stories, gifting us a culture in which we benefit from and enjoy each other's talents far more freely?

Exposing the other side of its sword, facing an unexplored domain in which few comparable revenue or profit flows preexist to place at risk, capitalism is all too anxious to exploit other fundamental innovations. Capital interests have launched with full force into the quest of making a profit from our expanding knowledge of the genetics of all life on Earth. Most scientists and ethicists agree that cures for genetic defects ought be sought, with appropriate caution and diligence. But capitalism does not systemically disincentivize development of dangerous or uncontrollable technologies if the liabilities of such are not clear, present, huge, and enforced. Not yet recognizing liabilities that are clear, present, huge, and enforced, capitalism hopes to make far more money on the genetic engineering of "goods" far less essential than cures for plagues.

Are non-reproducing grain seeds of value to humanity, simply because they require third-world farmers to repurchase seeds annually from western agribusiness? What about genetically engineered fruit with a carbonation fizz?

Are insect-resistant crops of use to humanity, when they may result in new crop-resistant insects somewhere down the road? Just because corporations can profit from the sale of allergen-free pet cats, ought that kind of meddling in the genome of Nature's five-billion year old tree of life be motivated by our economic system?

Have we examined the implications of opaque private interests of value arbitrage becoming primary guiding forces evolving the genetics of life on Earth?

Turning our attention away from such epic questions as hacking Earth's 5 billion-yearold tree of life merely to make a buck, it is important to point out how technology is equipping capital interests with capabilities that are not far removed from simple thievery, operating under the guise of savvy investment management. It is clear that increasing information systems integration within markets is equipping capital interests with profit-seeking software systems. One can think of current—and next-generation computer trading stations within investment management institutions somewhat like profit-seeking technology harnesses worn by their operators, integrating humans and machines in cybernetic collaboration, operating at fiber-optic speed and evolving mathematically complex, shorter—and longer-wavelength calculus (of which, by virtue of interaction effects, no individual human may even be conscious, including the designers and operators). This emergent capability may have the consequences of increasing mobility of capital, volatility of perceived asset value, and general churn (flow) among balances subject to even the most subtle asymmetries in information access facilitating an arbitrage—all of which has more to do with opaque private interests than the actual value of macroeconomic functioning to the typical human being.

This is particularly relevant to consider in the wakes of various global currency crises and the technology economy bubble, both the inflation and deflation of which could be used—and driven—by savvy investment professionals for gain. As pointed out by Francisco Gomes, associate professor of finance at the London Business School, in relation to the recent collapse of growth in the technology economy, " . . . in financial markets arbitrage is commonly conducted by a relatively small number of specialized professionals (such as hedge fund managers), who combine their knowledge with the resources of outside investors. In general, investors do not know or understand the strategies or specialist knowledge of the arbitrageurs (and arbitrageurs have no incentive to reveal such knowledge). This separation creates an asymmetric information problem, as arbitrageurs and their investors must make decisions based upon different degrees of information."[8]

High-tech integration of markets enables centers of wealth to acquire rising equities early, and to unload falling equities early onto the backs of less integrated decision-makers—most often small investors.

These defects in the structures and processes of capitalism—programmatically under-investing in tools that can free people from the need of its currency, while over-investing in tools that allow engineered opulence to become ever more extravagant, and employing technology to create, manipulate and leverage information asymmetries within economies—are becoming increasingly obvious in proportion to human experience and the powers emerging from science.

Surveying the pervasive structural problems resulting from defective metrics and out-ofcontrol wealth concentration, it can be seen how capitalism can often wield more power than democracy itself. The ultimate illustration of this imbalance of power can be seen in the manner in which capitalism maintains the ability to define financial "value" while denying democracy the same right. Several simple questions convey the significance of this concern:

Q   Why do markets measuring "Yahoo.com" today certify the existence of $Y billion in asset value (equity = leverageable benefit and control, considered a non-inflationary asset), while "SaveAfrica.org" can't? Compare the actual future value of their present functions.

Q Why do markets measuring "Merck" today certify the existence of $M billion in non-inflationary asset value, while "Cure AIDS" can't? Compare the actual future values of their present functions.

Q If "Philip Morris" can make millionaires through equity assets, why can't "Amazon Forest" make a regular, competitive payroll for preservation? Compare the actual future value of their present functions. One makes people feel a high from smoke, killing many in the process. The other sustains all life on Earth with oxygen. Is the answer that one equity security pays those who ensure its continuance, and the other doesn't, because it has no certified equity security other than land, respected by capitalism's notion of real estate only if privatized, thus to be acquired by private fiat or by private capital, and then "made productive"?

Q What does Wall Street formally say the Amazon rainforest is worth? Is it the equity value of whatever parts of it companies can incrementally arbitrage (Ps on P&Ls, and growth thereof)?

Q If a hunk of metal and plastic called a "car" has an asset value of $C, why does a human have an asset value of $0?

Through the lens of these comparisons, it is easy to see how neoliberal capitalism allows a consumer and equity market to certify value, but disallows democracy from doing so, except in the negative, through taxation, regulatory restraints and protections.

Neoliberal capitalism insists that any positive value certifications (new capitalizations) by a democracy routed to citizens or Nature are to be considered "inflationary"—dilution of purchasing power of private capital sums, deemed a "bad thing" regardless of cause, basis or method. So the public's democracy must tax labor and private wealth via always-contested formulae, and borrow money from private wealth, at interest rates set by private wealth, to obtain funds for social service functions. Obviously, such a model has been made to function up to this point in history, but that fact doesn't preclude the existence or necessity of superior paradigms for the sharing and circulation of wealth.

To see why the denial by capitalism of democracy's ability to certify economic value is deeply unethical, one need look no further than at any of the many permanent-valuecreating missions of the form function(pay-little)—> benefit-forever that don't get properly funded by the democracy married to capitalism.

Q How much perpetual benefit would accrue to human civilization from an economic birthright providing for every single child to be loved, sheltered, given a healthy diet by her family, and provided a complete education all the way through college? Would such benefit not represent real future value?

Q How much perpetual benefit would accrue to human civilization if we capitalized all required resources to aid in the restoration of Africa?

Q How much less expensive would it be for humanity to fund cures to major diseases by capitalizing competitive non-profit enterprises, which seek no patents on resulting intellectual property? Would the benefit of minimizing future cost of the regimens not represent real future value?

In overly simplified and coarse terms, society recognizes that healthy and happy human beings are more valuable economic assets than starving, desperate, undereducated ones, but capitalism doesn't account for the value creation process in as beneficent a manner as we would for, say, the invention of a useful new technology. If a software entrepreneur can write 100,000 lines of innovative code and "create" multiple billions of dollars of "asset value" out of nothing material, in cooperation with equity markets which are programmed to measure future financial "values", why is it that we cannot similarly recognize the creation of future value in the stewardship and mentorship of people and life overall, and distribute the resulting appreciation in present currency through money supply or asset rebalancing in compensation to those providing such service? Is it simply because the investors and customers benefiting from such value downstream are everyone, nowhere singly identified? Is it because there is not an identifiable private interest, but rather "only" an identifiable public interest? Is it possible that we have not recognized the value creation within society's collective stewardship and mentorship functions formally because we simply lack the construct of a collective financial statement that measures the sustainable well-being of the typical human being and other life?

Within the existing parameters established by capitalism, the funds even for pay-little>benefit-forever missions must come from friction-ridden, often opaque processes of taxation and borrowings from private, largely amoral "net worths". Thus many vital efforts that would clearly create future value don't get properly funded, when, in fact, such ethical missions could be described and conducted instead as value certifications of democracy, yielding democratic equity growth—growth in the asset value (benefit) of citizenship.

~

Throughout my observations to this point, I have been presenting an appraisal of systemic defects in the programmatic logic of capitalism. Many will argue that my characterizations are relative and subjective judgments of the here and now, and that we ought depend upon statistical evaluations seen in the broad stretch of time. Some may offer arguments like, say, 'since a lot more of us than at any time in history are living in temperate homes, eating decent food, moving about in wondrous vehicles and living productive, meaningful lives, we ought not criticize the design of the pyramid we're standing upon.' True enough. But then one must ask what the pyramid's blocks are made of.

Lost in the fragmented science and humanities curricula and aged delivery systems educating students otherwise used to Sony Playstation games is the sense of the staggering, indeed unimaginable beauty and preciousness of Nature's living beings, particularly human beings. Spiritual traditions from every age of human history and every land of our Cosmic blue-green coral reef speak to the intrinsic values, purposes and rights of every single human being, and of our 5 billion year-old tree of natural life. In recent centuries, science has substantiated bases for the egalitarian ethic that runs through such traditions, and democracies have increasingly kept the promise of the sacredness of life through the cultivation and enforcement of human rights. But economics has a long, long way yet to go to fully reflect the spiritual, scientific, and political dreams of the visionaries of human rights we most honor.

Chapter 3
Concerns of Rights and Nature

"We hold these truths to be self-evident: that all men are created equal;
that they are endowed by their creator with inherent and inalienable
rights; that among these are life, liberty, and the pursuit of happiness:
that to secure these rights, governments are instituted among men,
deriving their just powers from the consent of the governed; that
whenever any form of government becomes destructive of these ends,
it is the right of the people to alter or abolish it, & to institute new
government, laying it's powers in such form, as to them shall seem most
likely to effect their safety & happiness."

—Declaration of Independence of the United States of America

Life on Earth evolved for billions of years before Thomas Jefferson's archetypal words were infused into the vision of a nation. This vision has carried us far in the relatively few years since it sparked the birth of the greatest democratic framework the world has ever known. Once-theoretical visions that liberty and human rights would self-sustain in democracies of educated citizens have since been validated, and represent today the continuing quest of a maturing global civilization.

After millennia of conflicts among religious, political and economic paradigms culminating in decades of apocalyptic confrontation between technology-wielding states, some people believe that the greatest threat to liberty and individual human rights remains the deep and imminent risk of reversion to totalitarian control through autocratic or simply exceedingly obese government. In 1944 Frederick Hayek wrote a then-criticized, now-worshiped book on the epic debate among the politico-economic systems of democratic capitalism, socialism, nationalism, and communism and their variants, in the context of World War II. In prescient reference to some of the catastrophic dangers of centrally-planned social paradigms, he said in the Road to Serfdom:

"The most effective way of making everybody serve the single system of ends toward which the social plan is directed is to make everybody believe in those ends. To make a totalitarian system function efficiently, it is not enough that everybody should be forced to work for the same ends. It is essential that the people should come to regard them as their own ends. Although the beliefs must be chosen for the people and imposed upon them, they must become their beliefs, a generally accepted creed which makes the individuals as far as possible act spontaneously in the way the planner wants. If the feeling of oppression in totalitarian countries is in general much less acute than most people in liberal countries imagine, this is because the totalitarian governments succeed to a high degree in making people think as they want them to."[9]

Hayek's brilliant insights are supported by most highly regarded explorations of economic theory. The assertion that the capitalist system yields significantly greater individual liberties relative to those afforded through socialism and communism has been succinctly validated in the history of the 20th century. Capitalism's success, wholly dependent upon the most rugged democracy ever conceived by human beings, has played an essential contributing role in the fostering of unparalleled realizations of freedoms of conscience, speech, faith, equal consideration under the law, and economic opportunity held by citizens of the United States of America. The liberation of spirit, vitality of individual empowerment and unbelievable diversity of free enterprise have captured the imagination of the world's peoples, so much so that it is now hard to find a large nation anywhere whose citizens are not drawn to the hypothesis of life experience postulated to be sustained by capitalism. And thus, while I do not believe that capitalism represents the ideal economic paradigm, it is highly improbable and certainly unwise for humanity ever to step back from the highest vision of economic liberation—a vision which capitalism was intended to fulfill, however incapable it may be to do so.

Some people fear a return to totalitarian autocracy is more likely to come from automation. They believe that technology poses the greatest long term risk to the preservation of real human rights. They argue that machines will one day overthrow natural life on Earth, or perhaps that we will allow natural life to meld with machines such that the two become indistinguishable, as we slide down a slippery slope thinking that we're enjoying Santa's sleigh ride all the way.

There is some merit to this concern. Software will soon be packaged with most PCs that understands speech, can translate among languages, and can enable computing devices to speak with a voice quality indistinguishable from human chit-chat. Credit bureaus and other personal information brokers now often know more about us than we do. Computer chess games are available on cell phones that can outplay experts. Refrigerators are in development that will remind you what you need to buy at the grocery store. Some companies are exploring how to send nano-robots into our bloodstreams to cure disease. Hit movies and TV shows are featuring computer-generated acting talent, and others are featuring stories about mechanical robots "living" among humans, expressing emotions. Sony is selling boatloads of robot dogs, with ads saying "AIBO is a totally new kind of robot—it develops its own personality—different from any other AIBO in the world. It features a built-in stereo microphone, voice-recognition technology and speaker. This four-legged robot has 20 motorized joints that make its movements amazingly realistic. With time and encouragement AIBO can learn about 50 verbal commands. It has four senses and expresses a full range of emotions, too. The AIBO ERS-210 comes with . . . software called 'AIBO Life' that allows it to learn from its environment and human interaction, and to mature from infant to adult. AIBO has a strong desire to perform, to play with people and to move about. It's a true companion!" (One can speculate how long it will be before Coca-Cola sponsors Sony's AIBO to "bark" out a brand impression.)

Such wonders make for great entertainment, and indeed serious questions. Physicist and writer Stephen Hawking believes that "the danger is real that this [computer] intelligence will develop and take over the world," and goes so far as to suggest that we should engineer the human genome to advance our intellectual capacities while we are advancing the powers of computers, even connecting our brains to computers, so that we can stay ahead of them.10 While I believe that is a gravely mistaken solution to the problem, some of his underlying concerns are worth considering.

But as an expert in some domains of science and technology, I will suggest to you that it's not automation itself that we should be concerned about. I don't particularly fear that we will fail to figure out the rights future generations of robots ought to have, because we will face a similar question long before we can make androids of the sophistication portrayed in Spielberg's Artificial Intelligence. Here's why: capitalism's leading corporations are already cybernetic organisms. They're already "living" among us. They are intelligent, they are each programmed with very specific, rapidly-evolving code, and some of their parts—human beings and other animals—most definitely experience real emotions. What concerns me more than smart techno-pets that begin to eat our lunch is that modern corporations already are machines equipped, through human beings and exponentially-smartening microprocessors, with every intelligence, emotion, and capacity that we can imagine. And all large corporations share some common bits of programming, some common goals—dimensionally-defective motivations that I've reviewed previously in this essay.

Connecting these threads together is a simple, fundamental question: isn't the financial code of capitalism itself, guiding every decision of massive globalizing corporations equipped with every technology known, in many ways a state plan centrally dictating key parameters of the life experience of its citizens—its laborers and consumers? Isn't the P&L statement—the performance-determining code of capitalism—a kind of "central planner" with power over human lives comparable with the power of a nation-state? Does a common performance measurement system used by every one of its legal "persons" not constitute a central plan of a state with a different nature than the ones Hayek considered, a state nonetheless subjecting those within its jurisdiction to the goals and effects of its plan?

Let me be clear that I fully understand the value of universal currencies and objective, shared measurement systems; they enable vast diversities of productivities to emerge and integrate efficiently through free markets. My concern is how success is defined: capitalism sustains only those free-market productivities that advance its "amoral" central P&L and balance sheet plan. Consider Hayek's words in description of the tactics of the economic totalitarianism he so feared:

"[Making people think as totalitarian governments want them to] is, of course, brought about by the various forms of propaganda. Its technique is now so familiar that we need say little about it. The only point that needs to be stressed is that neither propaganda in itself nor the techniques employed are peculiar to totalitarianism and that what so completely changes its nature and effect in a totalitarian state is that all propaganda serves the same goal—that all the instruments of propaganda are co-ordinated to influence the individuals in the same direction and to produce the characteristic Gleichschaltung of all minds. As a result, the effect of propaganda in totalitarian countries is different not only in magnitude but in kind from that of the propaganda made for different ends by independent and competing agencies. If all the sources of current information are effectively under one single control, it is no longer a question of merely persuading the people of this or that. The skilful propagandist then has power to mold their minds in any direction he chooses, and even the most intelligent and independent people cannot entirely escape that influence if they are long isolated from all other sources of information."[11]

If we take Hayek's mental picture and replace the notion of human autocrats with balance sheets and profit and loss statements, and set their asset, revenue, profit and growth measures as the common planned goals of a "capitalist state", does Hayek's cautionary portrait not foretell of some of capitalism's present behaviors? Through massive public relations machineries and even more massive advertising industries, the neoliberal capitalist state reinforces everywhere the perception of the goodness of its ends and means; symptoms and characterizations of its badness are suppressed by code-driven system function, through the commercialization of news media, confidentiality imposed by proprietary information shelters, and the opacity of financial statements and markets built upon them. In the modern capitalist state, there is no human dictator commanding millions of followers; but there is nonetheless a dictating logic obeyed—even worshiped—by millions. Criticizing 'growth' in 2010 New York. is like criticizing Stalin in 1940 Moscow. Criticisms of 'profit' are deemed even worse, for they are not just curses at neoliberalism . . . they are blasphemies of capitalism.

Contemplating in 2010 concerns about capitalism similar to the concerns about state-run collectivisms that so moved Hayek, we are led to the philosophical point which drove the world towards capitalism in the first place: a more libertarian and egalitarian realization of economic well-being must become a human right in the fundamentals of political-economic code. We must ask ourselves—experientially equipped to do so for the first time only recently—what rights and functions cybernetic organisms we call "capital interests" ought have in relation to human beings and other life forms.

While many economists will beg to differ, economic well-being is not deemed to be a human right protected by the laws of democracy today. This fact is plainly revealed by the widening relative gap between rich and poor, and by other simple questions:

Q Has the leverage of automation built upon shoulders of centuries of science and labor become a democratic right of all people, through the reduction of the need to work?

Q Is the joy of art emerging through the visions of centuries of artists presently a democratic right of all people? Q Does society give a poor carpenter's daughter and a rich CEO's son even remotely comparable opportunities in life?

Q   By what right does one 21st century child inheriting assets deserve an arbitrarily larger inheritance than other 21st century children, when the inheritance is derived from collective science, art, enterprise, and technological automation?

Q   What are the root causes landing 2 million human beings in U.S. jails?

Q   How many orders of magnitude apart can the social investments in an African and American remain, if we truly intend to evolve an open and democratic world?

Q   Why is it that a Toyota can traverse national borders far more easily than a human being?

Q   Is it, in fact, right that a corporation—or simply a money-sum—can have legal status as a "person"?

Whatever the answers may be to these painfully fundamental questions, it is an indefensible obscenity to suggest that economic class today does not bound a newborn child's real freedoms, real opportunities, and real experiences in her future life. For any president, economist, or corporate executive to suggest in 2010 that the United States of America is fulfilling the hope of human rights and individual liberty that informed its constitution is at best a reflection of inexcusable ignorance, and at worse a terribly evil lie. Visit the poor center of any major city in the most "developed" part of the world—and ask yourself whether the people you see experience the kind of life, liberty and pursuit of happiness worthy of the U.S. constitution . . . or of humanity's potential.

Denial of responsibility for this painful truth does not make us innocent. It increases our guilt.

If we are ever to imagineer and then evolve into our economic system effective corrections to these defects, it is vital that we understand the depth of moral truth and dedication required of a new paradigm, and this understanding requires appreciation of the actual state of affairs of the typical human being today. What is revealed when we honestly examine the present life circumstance of the typical human being is just how far we have yet to go to enable the well-being of all life everywhere.

"If God had formed us of the stuff of the sun or the stars . . .
then we might have said our beginning was honorable . . .
But when someone is made of clay, who pays any attention to him?
Who are we? We are all made of mud, and this mud is not just on the hem
of our gown, or on the sole of our boots, or in our shoes.
We are full of it, we are nothing but mud and filth both
inside and outside."

—John Calvin

As we begin the third millennium, it is readily apparent that the emotional compasses of human beings everywhere are spinning. The reasons are complex and multifaceted, but one transformation stands out as a cause: human ontology has undergone a transformation during four centuries of the scientific revolution. The relative fall of primitive religious dogmas such as those expounded by Calvin has opened people to vital intellectual and physical freedoms, while also inadvertently diminishing faiths in intrinsic values. Though it does not yet express it in these terms, science has revealed that we are children of the Cosmos, spirit-like babies made literally of The Force of Stars, but science also is risking throwing life's sacredness out with dogmatic and ignorant religious bathwaters. In its vital quest to identify and label each thing for its distinctions, science has left modern Western culture deficient of awareness of just how beautifully and totally interconnected we are with each other and with Nature.

In giving every leaf its own name, have we forgotten that we grow from one tree?

With religions partially denuded of influence, and with science not yet expressing the integral Nature She reveals through the lens of physics, humanity's dependence upon the code of economics as the moral standard has grown—a role capitalism was not designed for and cannot fulfill. To any human being equipped with a heart, it is clear that many of the deepest values we hold cannot be expressed in terms of dollars, so if the dominant value system guiding society is capitalism, it is equally clear that many of our most deeply held values are not being served by society.

The signs of a deficiency of meaning and purpose in peoples' lives are everywhere: rising use of antidepressants of many kinds; kids shooting kids, unless they're drugged, spied upon, and metal-detected; Nature-lovers and believers in a simpler, egalitarian way of life finding it nearly impossible to function well within the system; protesters throwing rocks at presidents and prime ministers; civil wars killing millions over shiny bits of carbon; the inability of nations to find the middle ways for hot and cold wars to come to final rest in world peace.

Visionaries and activists are making transparently visible the incompatibilities between truly universal spiritual beliefs and capitalism—a forcing function that will become far more powerful than it was in Seattle or Davos or Genoa. More and more people are coming to believe that, beyond a certain threshold needed for a simple, healthy, diverse life, manufactured opulence isn't so enticing after all. And ironically, this trend of awakening results in a third deficit of meaning confronting a rising percentage of human beings worldwide: not only have old forms of religious practice ceased to offer spiritual nourishment, not only has science failed yet to express broadly a new form of spiritual nourishment while it unseats religion as the lens upon reality, but now many are coming to realize that the economy within which we are expected to function each day isn't something we can deeply believe in. To a significant, likely-to-rise percentage of people in both developed and developing nations, the notion of corporate profit cannot be equated to a meaning or purpose that reaches to the level of a spiritual passion. Particularly as negative effects of economic growth can be seen with increasing audiovisual fidelity, through a real-time global communications network.

Can our economy be evolved to incorporate scientific truth, universal spiritual values and fundamental ethics so intrinsically into its code that billions of dazzlingly intelligent and good-hearted people can throw themselves into their life work with passion and energy and fulfillment and purpose undimmed by ethical compromise? Can our economy be evolved to realize a world content not to grow its consumption beyond certain levels, a world content to let Adam Smith's opulence fall in some ways, a world able not only to avoid sinking into depression, but one forever risen from despair? Can our economy ever enable the true liberty we've sought throughout history, and yield honor back to Nature?

I hope so, for if humanity is to survive and thrive, it must.

~

Setting aside all these debates concerning this or that criticism of the logic and effects of capitalism, there exists a forcing function that appears to trump all other competing forces: it is clear that the needs of Nature and the interests of humanity's present economic paradigm are in mortal conflict.

Jeff Gates argues, "Unsustainable production methods are now standard practice worldwide, due largely to the worldwide embrace of a financial model that insists on maximizing net present value (that's largely what stock values represent). That stance routinely and richly rewards those who internalize gains and externalize costs (such as paying a living wage or cleaning up environmental toxins). That shareholder value-maximizing model signals executives to embrace manufacturing practices such that worldwide, as of 1996, the biologically productive area needed to produce the natural resources consumed and absorb the carbon dioxide emitted was 30 percent larger than the area available. This result reflects the key operational principle guiding neoliberalism: 'Maximize financial returns and, trust us, everything will work out fine.' U.S. money managers alone now invest $17 trillion in reliance on that mechanistic model. Just three U.S. investment managers now hold $1,900 billion that's 'managed' through an index such that the funds are invested in a portfolio of securities meant to mimic financial markets as a whole —what I call 'money on autopilot.' These huge sums are responsive to (and responsible to) only themselves because the current model assumes that any increase in finance-calibrated value contributes to the common good. This is the model we're insistent be spread abroad."[12]

Forests are disappearing. Fisheries are depleting. Oceans and lakes are being flooded with wastes. Aquifers are emptying. Weather patterns are shifting. Human numbers continue to climb. Earth's biosphere cannot sustain the existing footprint of civilization, with billions still in abject poverty. We are at the front end of what scientists now call the sixth great extinction. It is genocidal to lift the developing world into U.S.-style patterns of consumption using the 20th century's platform of technologies. Yet as of 2010, capitalism is programmed to do precisely that, and more than one billion people in China have just joined its program.

In dealing with resulting ecological crises, governments are presently able to put out increasingly frequent symptomatic fires through regulatory action, usually after flames reach critical temperatures, or otherwise after a sufficient number of voters have been scorched. But symptomatic remediation of environmental destruction is no longer adequate, as stressed by renowned scientist Paul Ehrlich: "Current trends in consumption and population cannot continue indefinitely. We need to look at the scale of the enterprise relative to the ability of life's support systems to continue in perpetuity. The scale of the human enterprise is a product of the number of people, how much each one consumes, and what kind of technologies are used to supply the consumption. Until everyone comprehends that, we will not have the kind of political action we need in order to survive."

We can explore the options we have to resolve systemically the ecological challenges we all face by expressing Ehrlich's statement as the equation: footprint = population x per-capita consumption / technology efficiency. To shrink humanity's footprint, we can either decrease the numerator or increase the denominator of the right-hand side of this equation, or both. Population is still growing and won't decline dramatically except in disaster. While we must work to stop growth in population, it's not a variable we can control sufficiently to make the needed difference in our footprint. If we fail to change our ways soon enough, Earth will likely reduce our population with brutal force, since that's the only factor in this equation She can alter to protect Her face from oily, polluting, wasteful footprints. Moving on to the next factor, consumption can't fall without sending capitalism into depression; letting consumption fall is an option, but only in the context of a more evolved economic paradigm which enables it to happen without sending humans into depression. And if we are to lift billions out of poverty at the same time, average consumption will probably increase even if it falls for the wealthiest people.

Thus, in combination with moderated population growth and consumption of material goods, we are left with one last option. Step-function increases in the environmental cleanliness and resource efficiency of our infrastructure and production technologies appear to be the most accessible courses of action, and are certainly an absolute prerequisite for any desirable solution to the challenge framed by this equation.

Here's the problem though: as I described above, capitalism won't aggressively support a technology from which it has difficulty sustaining a profit. Neoliberal capitalism doesn't value a device or service unless people pay an arbitrage to capital interests. Perhaps more importantly in this case, dominant forces within capitalism's wealth structure tend to suppress technologies and methodologies that would diminish the major revenue flows sustaining their dominance; these forces act to protect the revenue flows available for arbitrage. If a new tool costs little or offers free leverage, making obsolete a vast existing capital flow and political structure, how sure are you that its science and scientist are well-stewarded by capitalism today? For example, if we could, in fact, develop an energy-producing device that makes fossil fuels and their existing capital flow structure largely obsolete, do you really believe that capitalism is properly motivated to fund aggressive R&D and introduce it?

The economist will be quick to say, "yes, that's what entrepreneurs do: eat the lunch of entrenched competitors, by meeting needs in better ways and at lower costs." This is, of course, true in idealized competitive markets, and often in practice as well. But speaking from years of professional experience in precisely this quest, I can tell you that in this case the economist's belief is wrong. When we are talking about technologies so inexpensive and leveragable as to make obsolete significant fractions of the world's present economic activity, which technologies would also democratize the power structure of civilization as a whole, the debate shifts to a different level entirely. If the music industry can align all powers in its possession to obliterate Napster's liberation of songs, what might vastly larger interests do with energy and propulsion technology that would liberate electricity and transportation . . . and politics? The origins and continuing functions of the national security apparatus of the United States government deserve serious examination in this respect.[13]

If my speculations on the plausibility of such technologies prove true, then society is presently equipped with a needlessly wasteful and top-heavy infrastructure, significantly derived from physics that predates even a room-size calculator. The self-preservation instincts of the political and economic interests dependent upon this infrastructure may well have invited unconscious—and in some important cases conscious—dumbing-down of human beings and their democratic institutions in recent decades. Since election outcomes today correlate more to votes of capital than to votes of people, it is fair to say that in 2010, capital interests are sustaining at least one intellectual impairment within the helm of our democracy.[14]

Chapter 4
Concerns of Maps and Frontiers

"We are indeed approaching a culmination of sorts; our species seems to face a kind of test toward which basic forces of history have been moving us for millennia. It is a test of political imagination—of our ability to accept basic, necessary changes in structures of governance—but also a test of moral imagination."[15]

—Robert Wright

The field of economics has been criticized from time to time as excessively unscientific, lacking the precision and completeness achieved in some other domains of study, where models of cause and effect more fully describe structures and processes with great predictive power. My personal view is that these criticisms of economics are partially valid, but not for at least one of the reasons commonly expressed, namely that economics deals with complex systems with inherent chaotic functioning. This is obviously so, and thus it is hardly surprising that we can predict the future course of economic activity with only moderate success. Just because it's tough to predict the weather does not mean meteorology is not a science. Rather, meteorology, like economics, is a young discipline of study, still groping for fundamentals deeper than existing approximations, and forever grasping for integration of information sufficient to see otherwise invisible patterns spanning a vast constellation of short—and long-wavelength influences.

I would instead point out other deficiencies in the maps and frontiers employed within the theoretical toolbox of economics, which, consciously preserved or not, contribute significantly to its inability to realize solutions to pressing problems of the world.

First, I am concerned that the discipline of economics does not admit in its public posture or fully map within its models the effects upon many of the systems that it animates and leverages. One broadly-studied example is inadequate cost attribution in the use of natural resources by corporations16. Equally problematic, the invisible hand of capitalism exerts a staggeringly powerful influence on the functioning of our democracy, guiding every major decision and uncountable minor decisions affecting both the immediate experience and long-term trajectory of life on Earth. The effects are numerous, ranging from de facto denial of economic rights for billions of human beings, to natural resource giveaways, to government departments that institutionalize, preserve, and grow what might otherwise be smaller or more temporary mission-focused functions (militaryintelligence operations, for example), to grievously inequitable paradigms of taxation, to the irony in loud cries from capital interests objecting to "over-regulation" of industry by democratic government, while the very same interests are busy exercising more control over democratic governance than ever before. It must be asked how much our natural resources and democratic institutions have become tools of a capitalist autocracy.

The Bush administration provides daily, naked evidence of a troublingly deep infection in our democracy, and one hopes that wiser leaders abroad may hold the tiller firm in the direction of higher, better visions. In but one of many intellectual absurdities, Bush's assertion that international treaties beginning to deal aggressively with climate change are "not in our nation's economic interests" convicts our president of stunning ignorance. His repeated assertion is little different than saying, 'Doctor, the removal of this cancerous tumor is not in my body's interest, because the incision will hurt for a while.'

Our maps of economic theory also fail to recognize the incredible power of control wielded by capitalism through the technologies we've cultivated in recent decades. We must acknowledge that technologies literally have become limbs of action for corporations. Corporations can no longer be viewed simply as groups of human beings collaborating in the provision of goods and services. Corporations—primary organizational structures within capitalism—must be understood in 21st century economic terms as physical mechanisms evolving ever greater capacities for output through the leverage of assets, technology and information, with permanent but lessening dependence upon natural human life for input labor. With this perspective in mind, risks of contraction and opportunities for expansion of human liberties may both be seen.

If we wish to evolve economics consciously in directions that yield human beings greater liberty, equity, and environmental stability, then the studies and portraits mapping economics must deepen and broaden to reflect comprehension of the superbodies and superpowers which economic code now animates. I previewed above the name I propose for this broader field of study—*ideomechonomics*—and explore the notion further in *Part II* of this essay.

~

The final concern I'll mention about capitalism reveals one of the many reasons why perfecting our maps of economics is such a vital quest. Unknown to most economists, politicians, businesspeople, and indeed most scientists, current research in the domain of science fundamental to all other domains of science—physics—is strongly suggesting that a startlingly profound set of discoveries may soon be made relating to the nature of the medium we call "space" or "space-time". If these discoveries unfold in the direction suggested by research currently underway around the world, revealing that the "vacuum of space" is in fact an intense medium of energy, long-held assumptions regarding the limits of the technologies central to the infrastructure of civilization—the energy that powers all machines and the propulsion systems that enable us to move—will be swept away, and an astonishing array of ultra-efficient energy and transportation machines may begin to emerge.[17]

If my speculations on the possibility of such technologies prove true, then our economy may well be faced with the most intense period of evolution in the history of civilization. Such new categories of tools would be as profoundly transformative to 21st century civilization as fire was to ancient man: nonpolluting energy generators with no need for a grid; unlimited pure water from the ocean; silent, hovering vehicles that make congested freeways a stress of the past; noninvasive fields capable of eliminating harmful bacteria and viruses by targeting their electromagnetic geometries.

Further, the transformation we may face in coming years, rising from newly clear comprehension of the physics of our Nature, may include deeply profound insights into such questions as the existence of other intelligent life in the Universe, the history of the Universe itself, and our future within it. As world-renowned scientist Carl Sagan long ago envisioned, such knowledge could significantly evolve human civilization, certainly including the manner in which our economy functions, by maturing our senses of unity, spiritual wonder and ethical responsibilities, reflecting new awareness conferred on us by Cosmic self-discovery.

These observations raise the question of how well capitalism comprehends the frontiers we may actually face. How many economists are conscious of the ways in which science may soon change old rules, yielding abundance where there was once scarcity, and opening all kinds of new possibilities and frontiers? Do we have economic models that recognize how to deal with infinitely leveragable technology, like free energy? Would capitalism foster use of such technologies with the responsibility and wisdom they would clearly demand?

What happens if we realize one day that humans may be charged with evolving a stable economic paradigm for a civilization capable of spanning more than one planet?

Would we fix our cancerous models of growth before touching—or perhaps before being allowed to touch—other worlds?

Scenarios of the Future

"All told, our menu of options is rich, ranging from self- annihilation to graceful adaptation, and emphatically including the middle prospect of a long and turbulent adjustment full of strife and suffering. It is the destiny of our species—and this time I mean the inescapable destiny, not just the high likelihood—to choose."[18]

—Robert Wright

Coming back from futuristic frontiers to the very present reality of 2010, we must face with courage, compassion, and integrity both the total risk and historic opportunity following from the fact that our economy is an integrating global mechanism, upon which 6+ billion human beings are thoroughly dependent for survival. Protesters against globalization should note that the worldwide availability of an agreeable economic paradigm is a profound social value that must and can be distinguished from the less-than-agreeable neoliberal code currently driving such a high-stakes deployment across humanity's only blue-green planet. It is in the exploration of this distinction—between the values of a globally-available economy in contrast to the problems of modern capitalism—that serious intellectual engagement, governing realities and populist protest movements may align common action, advancing with clarity and focus the debate over the future of global economics through the union of wisdom, patience, logic and love.

Framing the real stakes of that epic debate, it is useful to sketch three scenarios depicting my present view of the range of future circumstances significantly determined by the trajectory of economics. I've listed these scenarios in order of preference.

1. **The softest launch possible:** We figure out together how to evolve our system in the first 20 years of this century, through a compassionate display of collective intellectual and spiritual aikido—slowly shedding

excess materialistic clothings of modern civilization, gradually realizing a social paradigm whose economy measures itself for true human liberties, ethics, equitable balances, stable cycles, environmental cleanliness, and the degree to which it can minimize its own necessity. We harness the awesome forces within the singularity into a loving, free, egalitarian, sustainable foundation. Homo noeticus may soar through an astoundingly beautiful Cosmic birth. Earth becomes again the garden we know She can be.

2. **A very hard landing**: We surrender modernity, letting top-heavy infrastructures collapse, rust and fall, retaining all the love, ethics, wisdom, knowledge, and experiences we've earned throughout history. We experience a long and very painful series of crises, combating provincialism wherever possible, as people rebuild distributed communities around democracy, science, spiritual traditions and egalitarian economic models.

3. **A catastrophic crash and possible rebirth**: Early 21st century civilization fails to cohere around visions and actions capable of evolving successfully the 20th century machine; a chaotic and devastating decay, revolution, and recovery occurs over centuries, if ever. Extinction of humanity is distinctly possible.

Of course, there is an infinite diversity of futures to which our paths may actually lead. But constraining consideration to this coarse spectrum, the first scenario would likely resonate with the hopes and dreams of most people; it certainly resonates with me. So how might we begin to take concrete steps to increase the likelihood of realizing a most beautiful future vision?

We can recognize the latent opportunity for a renaissance of human civilization staring us in the face: our economic system is a stunningly talented networked mechanism enabling humans to collaborate in the provision of goods and services to any place on the planet. We can leverage the fact that it's just now capable of decision-making and action at both individual and global levels. We can step up to the responsibilities that follow from knowing that systemic change of its direction involves wise and compassionate alterations of the momentum of our mass of interests. Capitalism guides these interests through every measure, contract, transaction, sponsorship, and investment. If we can figure out how to evolve properly the core code that guides our economy, we can redirect its tremendous capacities in remarkably coherent, effective ways—advancing society over the next several decades much closer to a stunningly utopian reality.

At an instinctive level, many people are sensing that a more compassionate, egalitarian kind of economy is indeed possible, one that can actually deliver the liberties promised by capitalism, and more. What would it be like to live in a democratic civilization whose economy honors and respects life intrinsically, fosters rather than destroys the diversity of cultures, sustains better balances between individual and shared interests, yields far more stable and equitable structures, and enables you to put to rest forever internal moral conflicts and external survival concerns relating to economic activity?

What would it be like to receive the right to the liberty of time, becoming truly free to choose creative and intellectual passions, missions of service, or whatever else you love as the focus for your day?

And what would it be like to be able to leave the doorway to your home unlocked at night, while you and all those you love sleep safely and soundly?

Part II
A 100-Year Vision of a More Sustainable, Egalitarian, and Libertarian Civilization

Part II of Evolving Economics sketches a larger context for the
modeling of macroeconomic activity. Long-term solutions are
outlined to correct fundamental defects in the neoliberal expression of
capitalism, defining a new *egalibertarian* economic system.
If successful, these solutions may fulfill the dream that
powered capitalism's ascent in the first place: to free economic
activity from the defects inherent in autocratic central plans.
By replacing the central plan of neoliberal capitalism—the
self-interested revenue and profit growth motive—with a
framework allowing far more diverse kinds of performance and
success metrics, we can enable measures of value and
productivity to index to any qualitative ideals established by
democracies of people. Within such a framework, a
new paradigm for the sharing of wealth becomes feasible.

If successful, the solutions proposed may eliminate the conflicts among
responsible visions of egalitarian, libertarian and sustainable society.

Chapter 5
Toward a More Evolved Economic Paradigm

"I doubt we will see a new coherent, universal ideological reaction to globalization—because I don't believe there is an ideology or program that can remove all of the brutality and destructiveness of capitalism and still produce steadily rising standards of living."[19]

—Thomas Friedman

To be sure, without a different economic paradigm that works, we cannot afford to change the one we have. But as argued in Part I of this monograph, we have the moral obligation—and the survival imperative—to realize a more evolved macroeconomic paradigm in coming decades.

Think of our economy as a Boeing jet in which 6+ billion human beings are traveling. This is a very special vehicle, because if it loses altitude beyond a certain level, it will crash, and the problems with our jetting economy are many. A small percentage of passengers enjoy a luxurious, spacious first class compartment, with every convenience imaginable just a call button away. Behind the shield of the first class compartment are billions of passengers in economy class, struggling day in and day out to put food on their seat-back trays. Billions more human beings are packed in the austere baggage compartment below, killing each other over food scraps and the right to sit in the economy section one day, if they're lucky. Meanwhile, our jet is programmed to continue flying—and feeding, sheltering, clothing and employing us all—only if it continues to gain altitude, and only if it is continually refueled and resupplied. But our vehicle was never programmed to understand that jet airplanes cannot gain altitude forever—they can only fly in a bounded atmosphere. What happens when the air is too thin to give our plane any further lift? Our vehicle is also built to consume fuel and supplies faster than they can be replaced naturally. What happens when these materials are gone?

The immense challenge we all face is that we have to reprogram our vehicle to fly at various altitudes with complete stability. We have to rebalance the seating arrangements before people become so desperate that they start destroying the hydraulics, or simply setting the fuel on fire. We have to reengineer major parts of this vehicle to consume far less fuel and supplies. We have to do all these things while still in flight . . . or develop a new vehicle with these qualities flying alongside the one we're in, and gradually move in to it.

Stepping up to this challenge in recent years, many great thinkers have contributed to our increasing comprehension of the systemic problems intrinsic within the prevailing economic paradigm, and have begun to propose serious strategies for dealing with these problems.

This community includes people like William Greider, piercing through the opacity of financial institutions and global economic processes, his investigative examinations offering a rare combination of rugged truth and pragmatic balance; Robert whose pragmatic intersection of present state of affairs and future responsibilities are highly regarded across the aisle; Paul Hawken and Amory and Hunter Lovins, proposing ways to integrate Nature-respecting values into the pricing of goods and services, enabling the true costs of resource utilization to be reflected and respected throughout economic activity; Thomas Grecko, whose studies "The Nature of Currencies and Credits"; Jeff Gates, whose empirical analyses of the defects of neoliberal capitalism are definitive, and whose ideas on redeployment of the assets of democracy to capitalize citizens represent essential steps on the path to an egalitarian and libertarian future; David Ellerman, whose insights into the realities and possibilities of economic development penetrate the fog of local and international politics and respect the realities of individual human behavior; and myriad others, like Hazel Henderson, revealing through indices the systemic social defects resulting from the neoliberal economic paradigm, raising awareness worldwide of the criticality and opportunity for basic change. There are many other writers and thinkers who are actively articulating and testing ways to leverage past learnings to deal effectively with future realities.

Following their lead, I would like to respectfully disagree with Thomas Friedman's assertion that no coherent post-capitalist vision of global trade is possible. I will sketch below a new, more egalitarian and libertarian vision of macroeconomic activity, in two steps. First, I will identify two cornerstone ideological shifts necessary for the rational conceptualization of a more evolved economic paradigm. Second, and in greater detail, I will present a series of specific changes to the practices of modern business which, together, may articulate the kind of transformation we seek.

The paradigm I sketch below aims to describe a democratically-equilibrated, Nature-respecting economy of free individuals and organizations. It's a sketch of a meta-system that could inform a new species of economy, combining the best qualities of existing paradigms with new qualities.

It is an outline of a meta-system inclusive of my present understanding of the *Ownership Solution*[20] and Natural Capitalism[21] models now becoming familiar to mainstream economists. The paradigm I describe—an *egalibertaria*—defines possible mechanisms of incremental evolution that can lead to a long-term transformation, envisionable now.

Shifting From Self-Interests to Shared Interests

"Each time I reason, each time I try to use logic,
I'm extremely pessimistic. When I use my heart, when I use my
faith—and I have a stainless faith in mankind—then I become optimistic.
A situation will arise that will awaken people, and we will suddenly
understand that we have to join forces."

—Jacques Cousteau

A common thread running through my criticisms of neoliberal capitalism is the notion of profit as an ethical avenue for self-interests to operate. I believe that evolving this notion is the first and most fundamental shift required of us.

It will be argued now, as it has been argued for centuries, that egalitarian and libertarian ideals inherently conflict with each other—that libertarian human nature is not compatible with the community-interest motive required by a truly egalitarian economic paradigm. It will be argued that the self-interest-driven paradigm institutionalized in the capitalism of 2010 is the only model appropriate for the foundation of human economic interaction. More precisely, one of the basic assertions likely to be fielded against the vision that follows is the notion that free market economic activity is inherently dependent upon the self-interest motive, both of which allegedly conflict with community-interest-driven economic activity.

In my view, the self-interest-driven priorities ascribed to instincts of human beings are thoroughly linked to the extrinsic life histories and social circumstances of individuals, and are not fixed traits of human beings as a species. The relative equanimity of civilization in spite of the depravity of effects of the prevailing self-interest-driven economic environment literally shouts out the depth of moral character within most members of the human family. I further assert that community-interest-driven economic activity is, in fact, the only form of economic activity that can sustain free markets over the long term.

While my assertions do not change the fact that billions of people are already well into the stretch of their extrinsic life experience and can be expected to change behaviors only gradually, I do maintain that changes to individual priorities are possible whose aggregate reach, coherence and consequence may be remarkable.

We hear rather often these days the contention that a more evolved economic paradigm must start through an internal change of heart within individuals, growing in coherence to catalyze significant external change. This is so true, but such change is linked in a simultaneous equation with the externalities that bound the feasibility and durability of changes in lifestyle and behavior. Capitalism in 2010 makes it damn tough for the ordinary worker even to perceive how he or she can establish new ways of living, let alone act upon such perceptions.

For macroeconomic change to occur, intrinsic and extrinsic change must take place in lockstep; neither is practical or sustainable without the other. We must be willing to change our ways, confident that the macrosystem around us will support rather than fight our will to change.

In short, we must recognize that fulfilling individual self-interests depends far more on the fulfillment of self-interests shared by all human beings. When we systematize this recognition, we will take a giant leap toward a brighter future. I will describe how this may be accomplished shortly.

Beyond this argument rests the simple fact that, regardless of the instincts evolution has produced within human beings, our future survival depends upon conscious evolution towards the kind of egalitarian and libertarian society herein contemplated. Perhaps as important, and setting aside merits of my particular future vision, our conscious evolution towards a new cooperative economic system can represent a new focus for the wondrous, beautiful talents and energies of people everywhere. As we come together to envision and make real the kind of civilization we'd all like to live within and bequeath to our children, we can find new purpose, meaning, and passion.

~

In addressing issues as fundamental as humanity's global economic paradigm, several basic scientific facts demand explicit acknowledgement: human beings are animals who've just recently ascended into sentience and consciousness. We best be humble before the degrees of both our intelligence and our ignorance. Our economy is an amalgamated, superposed reflection of the reality of our collective life circumstances. Our individual consciousnesses see more information than ever before, in one sense deadening, but also subtly sharpening multi-sensory discernment. Each of us is a tiny part of an immensely complex interconnected organism—each carrying forward a specific biological and cultural history, personal agendas, and every emotion from the most evil revulsion to the most compassionate universal love. Any successful evolution of macroeconomics will depend upon and must enable human beings—at every level of development—to overcome hates, greeds, fears and try and trust new ways and means of living.

Thus, one of the necessary steps in making practical a large-scale transformation of macroeconomic activity is to shine light upon the totality of the economic fabric of our lives. In the first part of this essay, I stressed the importance of expanding theories of economics to reflect more truthfully the behaviors of mechanisms influenced by economic activity. By raising the level at which we examine economic activity—seeing it not as an isolatable aspect of our daily lives, but rather as primary machinery by which civilization self-sustains—we can increase both comprehension and objectivity in appraising its vast operations.

I previewed the label I've proposed for a domain of study integrating economics with the physical reality that it animates: ideomechonomics. In definition, ideomechonomics describes a shared system created, evolved, and sustained by conscious beings of Nature, through which beings of Nature may serve each other and themselves.

A partial listing of elements connected in this definition, in three overall categories, include:

> *Nature* . . . people, animals, plants, land, resources, Earth, Sun, Milky Way, and the Cosmos as a whole. Nature possesses an ontological status of the order of God, a living reality that gives to and receives from the mechanisms it creates. Natural beings possess intrinsic values, rights and responsibilities, inclusive of those declared by philosophy of democratic constitution, framing social ideologies. Those familiar with Ken Wilber's Integral Model22 will note the fundamental status of Nature as possessing significance in both left-hand and right-hand quadrants.

Ideologies . . . paradigms such as *egalibertarianism* (proposed herein), democratic capitalism, socialism, and communism. Such paradigms represent integrations of protocols and patterns including behaviors, constitutions, laws, code, structures, roles, measures, equities, values, interests, contracts, rights, obligations, rewards, penalties, currencies and markets. Unlike Nature, ideologies are strictly models of action among conscious beings. Such models have no intrinsic purpose other than their operation in ideomechonomic systems. Ideological innovation comes along with Nature's integral visions and mechanisms enabling previously unrealized patterns of action.

Mechanisms . . . information such as art, data, knowledge, secrets, ideologies; devices that provide physical, chemical, biological, information, or rights leverage, or leverage of distance, time, or scale; and organizations such as governments, markets, corporations, unions, and missions. Mechanisms are realizations of models and patterns; they interact with Nature as defined by ideologies. Innovation comes along with new ideologies, mechanisms and changes in Nature. Those familiar with Ken Wilber's Integral Model will note the status of these elements as possessing significance in right-hand quadrants.

The civilization yielded by capitalism is an integration-in-operation of all elements across these three classifications, yet neoliberal theory does not truthfully account for its effects across these domains. I believe that any economic theory seriously proposed as a means to address fundamental crises faced by humanity must incorporate responsibility for its effects upon the physical reality it is proposed to animate. It is for this reason that I think of economic theory as a component of a larger model.

Some may object to the term *ideomechonomics* as a type-label for such a larger architecture, based upon the reasonable observation that the name suggests an emphasis upon the rule-based aspects of economic functioning, and less emphasis upon the ever-mysterious and unpredictable behaviors of organic systems woven throughout the fabrics and foundations of any large-scale community of living beings. From such a perspective, perhaps the term *ecomechonomics* may be a more appropriate expression of the synthesis of these elements. This alternative term is an acceptable framing of the systems I'm describing.

However, my selection of the term *ideomechonomics* intentionally attempts to stress the malleability of an economic system governed by conscious, intelligent constituents. Like never before in the history of human civilization, we have the ability and perspective to understand the impact of our actions, and thus it is incumbent upon us to formally recognize the roles played by ideologies in the system functioning of a civilization. If nothing else, the recognition as abstraction of the concepts by which we organize society is of vital significance, since prediction of and rational response to future circumstance depends in many ways upon objective detachment from the experiential subjectivity that guides day-to-day life. This capacity is one of the qualities that distinguishes humans from earlier species of animals. In short, our ability to consciously choose a different future vision as our goal depends upon our recognition of the pliability of behaviors otherwise assumed to be unchangeable.

Let us never forget that the human-created mechanisms through which we serve each other and ourselves are inventions of our imagination, which have no special ontological status except that which we unconsciously and consciously invest in them. These inventions of our imagination can be evolved in any manner that humanity collectively deems useful for the well-being of all natural life—if we have the intelligence, courage, will and compassion to do so.

Chapter 6
Realizing Egalibertaria

With this context in place, we can proceed to explore responsibly possible solutions to the fundamental crises produced by the neoliberal code of humanity's prevailing ideomechonomic system. With each of the four categories of concerns described in *Part I*, I have paired below outlines of possible corrective strategies.

Addressing Concerns of Measures and Balances

Make revenue, profit and growth thereof secondary measures within financial statements; enable an infinite diversity of qualitatively-dimensioned quantitative measures to become the primary metrics of the value, productivity and success of enterprises.

To the first overall concern—the consequences of the determinant of economic success being the degree of accumulation of a context-free currency—it is entirely possible for the performance measures of free enterprise to be reframed, moving from simple sums to indices of intelligent functions. We can replace the primacy of revenue and profit line items of an enterprise's P&L with new *dimensionalized metrics*—quantitative measures of qualitative performance relevant to the broad sector in which the enterprise competes. In the process, the meta-system, or code, determining the performance of free market enterprise can be more intelligently and ethically founded than is possible within the success metrics defined by the raw form of capitalism practiced today.

Imagine that primary measures motivating an automobile manufacturer are not simple sums of currency, but instead the degrees to which typical customers can use ultra-efficient, durable platforms for locomotion. Imagine that primary measures motivating a pharmaceutical enterprise are not simple sums of currency, but instead the percentage of people needing certain drugs who receive the required regimen at the lowest cost possible.

Consider the possibilities of formally incorporating a specific success measure into P&Ls across many industries: the degree to which a consumer of a good or service is freed from the need of labor. A dimensionalized metric respecting the labor interest in freedom from labor might be based upon the percentage of free time afforded in the 24-hour day and/or the 365-day year.

In the proposed paradigm, traditional scalar sums of currency as revenue and profit remain important as success metrics, but only to balance output prices with input costs, accommodating as cost, not 'profit', visible working capital margins sufficient for modest incentives and investment in development.

Through such a measurement paradigm, life-respecting qualities can become formally measured as indices: quantitative outputs of qualitatively-dimensioned functions. Input qualities can be reflected in indices of output functions within financial statements. The eventual result: we can replace the market-enforced mantra of "GROW!" with other patterns as our goals. Metrics of aggregation can evolve towards metrics of perfection. We can pay less attention to the heights of sand piles and start measuring the beauties of sand castles. We can go beyond measuring "wood" to distinguish "posts" from "trees". We can go beyond measuring "trees" to distinguish "plentiful" from "endangered". We can motivate fuel efficiency. We can slim down wasteful packaging. We can cleanse our air and water. Economics can evolve the ability to value stability or contraction (or any other qualitative measure), within a given domain of economic activity, as effectively as expansion. Financial statements—and all markets built upon them—can be transformed from referees of pissing contests into referees of perfection-measuring flow models, by changing the metrics of financial statements. (See note 23 for a vital comment on the necessity, but inadequacy, of real resource cost pricing of "Natural Capitalism" in fulfilling these kinds of objectives.)

In a real sense, we can do to capitalism what capitalism did to economies run by human autocrats: we can replace the single plan of the capitalist state—to grow unconscious sums of wealth—with infinitely diverse plans. These plans can motivate achievement of indices of conscious ratios and other intelligent functions respecting non-financial qualities. Information technology can enable near-zero-cost measurement of inputs to such multi-variable functions.

Consider the use of newly dimensionalized metrics to make transparently visible human labor arbitrage and the replacement of human labor with automation. Imagine that enterprises across all large-scale manufacturing industries formally report in their financial statements the human labor statistics of their operations. Consider what may follow from (1) formally tracking and distinguishing the nature of inputs used in production of outputs, (2) formally motivating enterprises to minimize use of human labor and maximize the wages paid to human labor employed, and (3) formally motivating minimization of prices, not just through price competition but through enterprise missions and employee incentives, thus regarding falling revenue as problematic only with respect to actual cost structures. I believe that the utopian ideals we've dreamed about could finally find a way to operate throughout the economy as a whole. Prices could begin to fall to far lower thresholds, labor arbitrage could begin a steady decline, workweeks could begin a steady decline, and yet standards of living could begin a steady climb.

In such an economic paradigm, after a community relieves endemic poverty, starvation, health crises, and the basics of a good living for its members, a "zero-growth" condition of its economy would no longer represent disaster . . . it would represent success. We would hear no more of pundits' cries about a "stagnant, failing, depressive, unemployment-ridden" economy; we would instead hear about the vitality, efficiency, full-employment and sustainability of our economy.

New Structures and Processes

Evolve a new meta-system for the formation, capitalization, operation and measurement of free-market enterprises.

These notions beg the question of the meta-organizational paradigm in which such qualitative measurement systems can be established and maintained equitably, with necessary scalability and common, efficient, horizontal interpretability, and yet without the need for massive governing apparatus.

Today's capitalist enterprises function as efficiently as they do in part due to two foundations: an enforced and relatively stable system of laws and regulations which govern structures, operations, interactions, and reporting, and systems of consumer and financial markets which are able to measure implicitly and explicitly the competitive performance of enterprises in comparison to each other. Both of these foundations are essential to the efficient functioning of a modern free-market economy.

Imagine a more evolved corporate structure, instituted in law and reflected in the protocols of whatever kinds of markets actually needed by the future, admitting new classifications of participants. Imagine a stable economy of employee-controlled mission-focused Organizations that do not seek the conventional notion of profit. Democracy could define through Charters the classifications of allowed forms of such Organizations. Some Charters would regulate at the generalized level of, say, "C corporations" while other Charters would regulate at the specialized level of, say, "Cure AIDS".

In such an economy, Charters may explicitly and implicitly frame markets of producers and consumers. A Charter may set forth the transparently visible categorical framework within which relevant Organizations operate and are measured for success, while each Organization may express its free enterprise function in an Organization Plan whose measurement transparency (reporting requirements) is framed by its surrounding Charter and augmented by its Plan. An Organization Plan may set forth a visible operating model, based upon Charter-defined functions of dimensionalized metrics and Plan-specific additions of other functions.

Within the economy proposed, a new profit and loss statement would emerge: a 'Statement of Operations' would report 'Balance of Flows' indices of functions defined by the surrounding Charter and Plan. Charters would define metric functions required within a Statement of Operations, and Organization Plans would add other measurement functions. In a Balance of Flows statement, the conventional motivation of "profit" would dissolve to zero; Organizations would not seek or reward financial arbitrage; working capital balance functions for modest incentives and ongoing development activities would be defined in Charters and Plans as future investment expense accounts, allocated as part of costs. In a Balance of Flows statement, the conventional notion of "revenue" would resolve to equal the totality of costs, or, in other words, the currency required to replace the goods, services and resources employed (respecting proper resource accounting), plus future investment expense accounts. Organization Charters and Plans would motivate cost efficiency (and all other goals) through the ethic of a new macroeconomic vision, aligned with appropriate incentive compensation, which itself would be explicitly and openly included as a cost. All the while, such an economy would sustain free-market, mission-focused competition.

Thus, there would be no extrinsic motivation to grow revenue or profit simply for the sake of "Grow!" Since Organizations would not be whipped by external forces to grow sums of aggregate currency flow or value arbitrage just for the sake of private interests, the leverage of any kind of automation could flow directly to reduce prices; infinitely leverageable technologies could thus drop prices toward zero, and the most important equity that every human should own equally—scientific knowledge of Their Nature—could come to be reflected in prices of goods and services. An individual's purchasing power could thus increase with shared rights in the efficiency (the closeness to zero of prices, even though they reduce revenue flows) of the output of democratically-chartered, free-market organizations. Reductions in revenue flow attributable to better efficiencies or lesser needs would no longer be cause for any kind of alarm, rather they would be cause for joy.

Motivations to scale in any direction could be provided by Charter and Organization Plan dimensionalized metrics qualitatively characterizing objectives (such as 'eliminate poverty, make energy nearly free, sustainably', etc.), rather than depending on dimension-deficient, scalar or meaningless-vector measures of "revenue" or "profit" to somehow motivate good behavior. Rather than depending day-to-day upon government rules and restrictions to protect labor, Balances of Flows may enable business to measure its own success by an objective of lowering to a better level the average number of hours the typical human being needs to work each year. Within such a paradigm, we might, over decades, end the immoral arbitrage of people.

By making qualitative functions the primary success determinants in operating statements, measures of "better" performance can really mean better performance, and "worse" performance can really mean worse performance. Free-market business activity finally may become assessed in terms of human—and life-respecting values.

Consider the example of General Motors. Imagine that the Charter driving the transportation industry establishes the objective that success (and employee honor and compensation) is measured by the typical consumer's mobility needs being served by the least expensive, most efficient, and most sustainable means. What kinds of transformations would such a motivation system naturally foster? Rapidly reduced prices for locomotion, rapidly increased investments in mass-transit, rapidly reduced environmental pollution, and rapidly rising durability for the infrastructure produced by the industry.

Consider the example of Merck. Imagine that the Charter driving the pharmaceutical industry establishes the objective that success (and employee honor and compensation) is measured by the typical consumer's health needs being served by the least expensive, most efficient, and most sustainable means. The transformations naturally fostered by such a motivation system would include rapidly decreasing prices for drugs, continuation of the drive for innovation of effective therapies, and a rapid rise in attention to noninvasive, inexpensive, natural regimens to chronic health problems.

Consider the example of Pacific Gas and Electric. Imagine that the Charter driving the energy industry establishes the objective that success (and employee honor and compensation) is measured by the typical consumer's electricity needs being served by the least expensive, most efficient, and most sustainable means. The transformations naturally fostered by such a motivation system would include rapidly decreasing prices for electricity, escalation of the drive for innovation in energy generation technology, and a rapid rise in the environmental sensitivity of energy infrastructure. *It is intuitively clear that an energy enterprise which can deliver clean electricity to a million people at the cost of ten dollars per month per consumer is more valuable to humanity than one that delivers electricity to a million people at the cost of one hundred dollars per month per consumer; the proposed model identifies corrections to neoliberal economics to reflect this fact.*

Consider the example of CBS. Imagine that the Charter driving the news media industry establishes the objective that success (and employee honor and compensation) is measured by the typical awareness of the typical citizen of local and world affairs, accomplished by the least expensive, most efficient, and most sustainable means. The transformations naturally fostered by such a motivation system would include rapidly rising awareness of the citizenry, rebalancing of air time to better reflect relative importance of information, decreasing prices for media access, and escalation of the drive for innovation in communications and presentation.

Of course, many enterprises, particularly small businesses, likely cannot reasonably be categorized into industries able to be framed by specific Charters. Thus, for a significant percentage of commercial entities, horizontal Charters which frame general corporate law would govern—analogous to the structures framing C and S corporations and partnerships in U.S. commercial code. The operation of businesses under such law would reflect two significant evolutions from existing practices, among perhaps other evolutions: (1) the growth of revenue and profit would become secondary measures to the minimization of the labor time reflected in the unit price of the goods or services offered; in this manner, the economy as a whole becomes motivated primarily to increase the liberty of its consumers through reduction of unit prices, and consequent reduction of the need for subsistence-driven work, with far less regard of the impact of such price reductions to gross revenue; and (2) sustainability of resource utilization would become a primary measure of success, enabling consumers to direct their business to those Organizations that most respect Nature.

In simpler terms, the Statements of Operations of all businesses can turn into "consumer reports" voluntarily displayed at every door, desk and web site. The businesspeople who most effectively fulfill admired and valued qualities would naturally become the individuals most honored and rewarded by such a system.

In the proposed paradigm, arbitrarily-specializable Organizations can be measured in a commonly visible way. People can found Organizations freely, and join/leave them freely. No governing apparatus is required larger than existing governing apparatus. As within traditional capitalism, consumption, production, employment and wages remain determined by supply and demand. And a fundamentally new objective can be incorporated into the success metrics of economic functioning: the leverage of automation can be passed along to individuals through dramatic reductions in prices, liberating "overcapacity" to serve humanity as a whole. By removing the absolute growth of simple revenue and profit sums as the primary determinants of incentives and corporate value, we may unleash the benefit of science to enable the liberty and egalitarian well-being of human beings and Nature.

Indeed, we can come to measure the success of the economy not by how much capital private interests acquire, but rather by how little we each need to turn over the economy's living capital. This point is essential to understanding the possible merit of the proposed economic model: we may finally discover a viable means to translate the benefits of modernity into a utopian ideal of freedom from de jure (communist) or de facto (capitalist) forced labor, through the systematic reduction of average work weeks, enabling genuinely voluntary work to become, over decades, the dominant force in productivity.

And thus, a Statement of Operations with its Balance of Flows can become the fully transparent, visible basis by which external performance measures are aligned with internal performance measures. Any markets, credit systems, or other types of commissions that may oversee and compare Organizations by value may respect the same Statement of Operations respected by Organization members (employees) and customers.

As important, both human political democracy and science—a democracy of Nature—can be reflected in the frameworks of economic processes. Transparently-visible Charters and Plans can over time reduce dependence upon the chaotic, authoritarian and poorly-enforced regulatory apparatus that currently serve purposes of protecting human rights, environmental cleanliness, and overall ethics of corporate activity. In fact, I expect that Organizations would naturally come to compete with each other explicitly in terms of how many qualitative ideals they can fulfill.

Expanding upon this line of reasoning, consider the application of this model to the operation and financing of government functions. What might be accomplished by formally separating the allocation of funds for collective social functions from the operational fulfillment of such functions? What if a democratically-governed society allocated funds to Charters, and enabled fulfillment of Charter functions by Charter-certified free-market Organizations, measuring success of fulfillment in terms of dimensionalized metrics as described above? Might we gain both efficiency and efficacy by enabling a multitude of free-market, not-for-profit organizations to compete in the fulfillment of day-to-day functions of many of our overweight, self-perpetuating government bureaucracies?

What kind of government apparatus may evolve if it is programmed explicitly, economically, to minimize its own necessity through the successful, measured fulfillment of its functions? I dare speculate a significantly smaller, more intelligent, more successful government apparatus.

~

While the reformulation of corporate charters and financial statements represents a potentially far-reaching and systemic means of transforming macroeconomic activity, such a step by itself is not likely adequate to enable the kind of economic paradigm required by humanity's long-term future. Another category of change likely required involves the methods by which we share benefits and responsibilities throughout society.

I discussed above the question of the equity of capital and property distribution as enforced by capitalism, particularly the consequences of the fact that capitalism allows consumers and markets to establish asset value but disallows democracy from doing so. At a basic level, I believe democracies should have the power, employed only with super-majority authority and transparently-visible parameters, to certify and decertify the economic value of an entity or initiative involved within the economic system. While it has long been asserted, with significant supporting evidence, that enabling government to issue currency or otherwise create assets yields an unstable economy, I see no reason in principle why this need be so, particularly given that we live in an era, unlike the past, in which our ability to measure currency and asset quantities and flows has been refined by several orders of magnitude, and in which automation has fundamentally changed the nature of work.

There are many ways a democracy could certify economic value. The simplest among them might be to 'print currency' to be used for specific functions, functions defined by their Charters in terms of value-creation ends and means, success metrics to be tabulated over time. The significant implications of this to our monetary system are briefly discussed later in this essay.

Consider the possibilities of such a model. Imagine that a super-majority of the democracy chooses to certify the creation of social service vouchers as birthrights, sans taxation. Perhaps called "Life Cards", such vouchers might, among other things, fund the fulfillment of kindergarten through college education for every child. Imagine that democracy certifies the currency required to fund a crash effort to find a cure for AIDS. I would challenge any rational economist to seriously defend the notion that such value certifications are unjustified by their collective return on investment. Sure, such certifications will increase the money supply (at least within the current monetary system; an alternative is presented later). One can perceive and declare such as injurious to preexisting private capital interests, or one can perceive and declare such certifications as representing the creation of accretive wealth reflecting the real rebalancing of qualitative value produced by such certifications, not unlike how commercial market caps reflect the creation and relative balancing of private asset wealth.

In this sense, I am essentially proposing that we capitalize human beings directly. If a machine is an asset, then surely a human is as well, regardless of whether his or her output is arbitraged.

Another option for the certification of financial value for the benefit of ordinary citizens may be found in the declaration of equity value in natural resources and certain democratically endorsed missions as publicly-held assets24. Imagine that the Amazon rainforest is certified, by some kind of democracy of worldwide representation, to possess ten trillion dollars of asset value (a number I pull simply out of thinning air) indexed to the rainforest's integrity. What are the protective and restorative functions that might be financed by such a capitalization? How might such a capitalization transform the national economies whose livelihoods are presently hitched to the progressive cannibalization of this irreplaceable natural resource?

Whatever the means, why can't democracy judiciously, truthfully project the future asset value of a social mission, and allow currency or equity value to be issued from or borrowed against the certification? The argument that such actions always result in real dilution of the value of capital held by private interests is specious, or at best myopic. The egalitarian and libertarian well-being of humanity and life in general are not merely pleas in activists' manifestos; they are the real measures of the contextual, subjective value of any real form of capital, and are the determinants of actual economic health. The certification of economic value, through currency creation or asset recognition, need be recorded as a "bad investment"—yielding inflation in the pejorative sense—only if the funded mission fails to achieve its qualitative objective.

While money does not grow on trees, value does. Why can't we formally certify the existence of such value, without depending upon the destructive intermediary of arbitrage to do so?

One of the ways in which this kind of value certification could take place might be through the formalization of a new kind of financial instrument—perhaps called a Development Charter—enabling democracy to issue (and thus rebalance) currency to those who provide *pay-once->benefit-forever* development services. In traditional terms, if such an investment is successful, it need not be considered inflationary in the pejorative sense; it is directly analogous to a present grant of future "market cap", used to develop the permanent increase and/or rebalancing of social well-being or productivity defining the "market cap". The difference is that the economic justification of the Development Charter is measured in dimensions of life-respecting values, and the economic justification of the commercial market cap is measured in the dimension of wealth flow to private interests.

The Development Charter concept might represent a new populist notion that could change the real politick calculus currently blocking funding of urgent social missions of the form function(pay once)—> benefit forever. It can be viewed as compassionate and Nature-respecting monetary policy.

Extending the concept to perhaps equally controversial but less radical changes to the present means of social investment, we might replace our outrageously complex and unwieldy taxation process with currency issues for all pay-once-benefit-once social services. In traditional terms, such issues would be inflationary, diluting personal net worths as taxation does, but much more simply operated; a democratic vote to fund with new money a collective service of the form function *(pay-once)->benefit-once* is equivalent to a flat tax. Social Security, Defense, Prescription Drugs and others such investments in social well-being fall into this category.

Overall, democracies might establish these "Charter Trusts" through which to fund social functions, in two ways:

- ➤ To Organizations by proxy through individuals (social service vouchers), recipients given the ability to purchase social services from Organizations of qualifying Charter and qualifying Plan; the "Charter for Education", "Charter for Health Care", "Charter to Restore Africa" might be examples in this methodology.
- ➤ To Organizations that directly compete and qualify for ongoing fulfillment of Charter programs; the "Charter for Science" and "Charter for Defense" might be examples in this methodology.

We might thus fulfill democracy's social functions through competitive, ethically-founded, transparently-run Organizations instead of opaque, arthritic, self-perpetuating and monopolistic state-bureaucratized departments. The significant currency implications of such approaches to social service investments are briefly discussed later in this essay.

In any case, ideally, no issuance of currency or certification of assets by a democracy need be considered inequitable. Ideally, democratic certifications and distributions of financial value simply represent the equilibration of capital flows and asset ownerships in patterns that respect productive capacities, collective interests and egalitarian and libertarian rights. In the proposed paradigm, certain species of "inflation" and "deflation" can be evolved towards concepts of "changes in relative balances of value". Inflation need be considered pejorative only if it is abused or if it cannot be controlled, which, of course, are significant risks that must be monitored and managed with extreme care.

~

One of the questions on which I've been largely silent up to this point is the role of corporate equities, capital funds, and securities markets in the proposed economic paradigm.

Corporate equities and their markets are neoliberism's way of measuring and comparing the value and efficacy of organizations, forming an information matrix that is used to justify and govern the economy's system of private capitalization and return on investment. Obviously, capitalization of enterprises is essential to their ability to form, grow and evolve. In the proposed paradigm, the function of capitalization would operate at two levels.

At the macroscopic level, with respect to the financing of industry-growing development efforts in any domain (transportation, energy, information technology, health care, education, etc.), Development Charters would be established by super-majorities of the democracy, certifying funds of currency, allocating such capital to the classes of Organizations with qualifying Plans and credentials (which may include historical performance benchmarks or any other qualifications determined by governing Charters).

As one can infer in the above scenario, a great heresy is proposed in this economic paradigm: the traditional concept of private ownership of corporate equity would become irrelevant, as private interests would not "own" Organizations. Neither would the democracy, but the burden and benefit of capitalization functions of corporate equity would partially shift to the democracy. And the competitive-performance-driving influence of today's corporate security markets clearly would be rendered redundant by the transformation of financial statements described above, aligning competitive business behavior with the human-value-centered purpose and ethics of the overall economic paradigm.

So what kind of work would investment professionals find? Investment and venture capital funds of today's capitalism might morph into a new class of free-market Organizations themselves, Chartered to administrate the public capitalization process—deployment and oversight of Development Charter funds certified by the democracy. Development Organizations would lend or grant development capital based upon various measures of credit-or investment-worthiness. The mission of these Organizations would be profoundly important: catalyze the development and perfection of free-market Organizations within their domain(s) of expertise; measure the competitive performance of those Organizations; measure conformance to the democracy's Charters; make good decisions in deploying the democracy's value certifications.

At the more tactical, day-to-day level of capitalization, all Organizations would be free to define within their Plans the portion of revenue which they require as capital to pay incentives and invest in ongoing and future development activities. These funds would be fully administered by the Organizations themselves, as they are in today's enterprises. Their efficacy of investment would be reported along with all other important metrics in Organizations' transparently-visible Statements of Operations.

More important than these specific ideas, an egalibertarian economy contemplates that systems of equities, funds, and markets thereof need exist only as required to form an equitable and transparent meta-system sufficient to enable a comprehensive and stable capitalization system, a system fully true to the dimensionalized metrics which drive Organizations. It is not yet entirely clear to me precisely which existing capitalist equities, funds, and securities markets serve *necessary* roles that could not be fulfilled by the constructs described above. But it is plainly evident that some existing securities infrastructures serve roles that would be unnecessary or exposed as unethical in the proposed paradigm. In an egalibertarian economy, so long as the capitalization function is well facilitated otherwise, I see no right or role for corporations to operate simply to use private-interest-rewarding value attributions of organizations in massive systems of Vegas-style gambling, with no more meaningful objective than snagging an arbitrage.

In an egalibertarian economy, all forms of arbitrage are deemed unethical, as is the quest for profit beyond modest incentive and future investment in useful and genuinely sustainable development.

Respecting Rights and Nature

Realign economic law and monetary systems to facilitate and sustain broader rights of human beings and Nature.

One of the fundamental themes recurrent throughout this essay suggests that the status of the human being and other forms of life within the code of present-day capitalism does not do justice to the rights that they ought hold. The evidence for this is myriad: the despicable state of our education infrastructure, the unsustainability of our retirement system in the face of an aging population, the immoral consequences of our emphasis in law enforcement apparatus upon symptomatic rather than causative agents of crime, the commercial assault on environmental sustainability, the entirely irrational investment of hundreds of billions annually in "military security" rather than social security, and simply, fundamentally, the harnessing of billions of human beings to the yokes of enrichment strategies for a few million human beings.

Staring down such awesome challenges as these will require that we recommit ourselves to an aspiration which originally inspired the development of democracies, and capitalism, in the first instance: economic rights—the most fundamental of which is liberty from any kind of forced labor, de jure and de facto—must become deemed to be human rights. If we fail to step up to this challenge, I believe that we will seal the fate of modern civilization to experience a devastating period of decay and chaotic revolutions.

The strategies proposed above sketch means to completely restructure the purposes and ethics of macroeconomic activity. In principle, they would enable democracies of people—large and small—to align business operations with human—and Nature-respecting values, motivating free enterprise to sustain the rights and needs of life.

Two additional strategies come to mind to address this concern at a basic level. Both of them will no doubt be received by die-hard neoliberal capitalists with the same skepticism and revulsion which likely greeted some of the ideas floated above.

The first strategy squarely tackles the question of intellectual property, and the strategy thoroughly depends upon the notion that a democracy may certify the existence of economic asset value. I propose that we develop the economic protocols and infrastructure enabling most intellectual property to be accessed and used freely.

I propose that we do away with copyrights and patents over time. The democracy can establish a new legal construct—perhaps called a formright—to replace them, enabling the retention of rights of integrity and physical stewardship in the hands of originators.

With respect to creative works, a Charter for Culture could reward artists according to a dimensionalized metric of acknowledgement by people, through democratically-defined function-driven certifications of value (presumably in the form of issuances of new currency). One can call this "inflation", or one can say, "society will make art free by creating currency to recognize its intrinsic, incremental asset value". Development Organizations under this Charter can provide funding to worthy artists. Through such a system, society can stop arbitraging writers, artists and their creative works.

With respect to inventions, a Charter for Science could reward researchers and inventors according to a dimensionalized metric of the service leverage provided by their work, through democratically-defined function-driven issuances of currency. One can call this "inflation", or one can say "society with make useful technology free by creating currency to recognize its intrinsic, incremental asset value". Development Organizations under this Charter can provide funding to worthy projects. Through such a system, society can stop arbitraging scientists, knowledge and technologies.

Consider an example: a writer wishes to publish a book. Today, she will scratch and dig for her next buck. She'll write her first book during leisure time. She'll search for a publisher willing to bet on her. They'll release and market the volume, and wait to see how many people can afford $15 for her ideas. A few hundred thousand readers will read it soon if it's a best seller, and a limited number will do so across the future. She'll receive a small fraction of the resulting dollars.

Now consider the new paradigm: she will still scratch and dig for her next buck. She'll still write her first book during leisure time. She'll still search for a publisher willing to bet on her. But when they release and market the volume, anyone who is interested in the domain can read her work. If it has value, a few million readers will read it soon, and any number across the future will do so as well. Her income—and the income of her publisher—will be based upon use by people of her work.

Clearly, a key to making this notion work is to be found in the formulation of the dimensionalized metrics and the systems that employ them—a tough challenge indeed—and a stable system for interpreting inflation in fundamentally new ways. But this vision seems far less difficult to implement and far more compelling than bottling up something that wants to be free, scanning every email message for stolen IP, and securing (then securitizing!) every CD, screen, speaker, and keyboard in existence, withholding medical cures from people who need them, and brutalizing billions of human beings in developing nations through the IP-legacy-asymmetric "competition" contemplated by WTO-enforced free trade.

Obviously, a massive transformation of the architecture of our economy is proposed, for which voluminous analytical texts and studies must and will be developed. But it is the kind of general transformation that, I believe, is necessary and consistent with the scale of change required if we truly wish to evolve one day a sustainable, egalitarian, and libertarian society. When society gifts the conscious beings of Nature the right to use responsibly the arts and sciences of their Nature, we will spring refined culture and new levels of technological efficiency from the cage of capitalism's selfish, destructive and polluting arbitrage. We will take an important next step down the path of forever ending economic enslavement and restoring the organic health of life on Earth.

~

I pause before introducing a second strategy for dealing with the fundamental challenges of reprogramming economics to respect the rights of life, because of the knee-jerk hysterics and semi-rational hand waving that have confronted similar ideas in recent decades. I will also stress that this particular strategy requires a great deal of further work. But something along the lines of what

I am about to propose is essential to perfect, and in the face of challenges confronting the very survival of modern civilization, all ideas deserve to be aired in the spirit of well-intentioned and sober dialogue.

The idea follows primarily from the need to reinterpret inflation and deflation in new ways if democracies assume expanded rights to issue currency or otherwise certify and rebalance asset value. If new vehicles of currency creation, calculation, and wealth balancing are introduced—tools I believe must be developed—then means by which we can simply, reliably and ubiquitously manage the reinterpretation of certain species of inflation and deflation are essential prerequisites. In order to do this, we must become able to measure values in both absolute and relative terms—we must become equipped to measure sums of currency as ratios to total currency, weaning us off our dependence upon dumb sums alone as meters of value.

The notion is this: it might be useful to evaluate the merits of introducing a labor-time-denominated electronic currency through which to mediate economic activity.

Contrast the scenarios in which an undimensionalized medium—such as the dollar—is employed as the economy's currency, compared to the use of an electronic currency with a qualitatively-meaningful dimension of denomination.

Consider the functional attributes of the *dollar*. The dollar is an undimensionalized currency whose denomination value changes over time, generally losing denomination value over time. Its denomination gains or loses purchasing power with deflation and inflation respectively. A sum of dollars does not fluctuate with inflation and deflation; prices and wages fluctuate with inflation and deflation. No envelope, information, or trail may cheaply and reliably ride along with a quantity of the currency; as of 2010, these must be (expensively) institutionally-enforced.

Now, consider the possible attributes of a *labor-time-denominated electronic currency*, perhaps called a *time credit*. A time credit would be legal tender among Organizations, exchangeable with the dollar. The time credit would be a dimensionalized currency whose duration-denominated relative value (say, 1 minimum-wage hour) does not change; an individual's purchasing power expressed in terms of time credits would be indexed in real time to how many hours of minimum-wage labor time the balance affords within the macroeconomy. In such a monetary system, the qualitative value of the denominational unit of the currency may remain constant, and would be simply and intuitively meaningful to all people.

Your wage would become a measure of the relative value of your labor time to the economy as a whole, as a multiple of minimum wage labor (wage = credits/hour of labor), multiple freely determined by supply and demand. The price of a good or service would relate to how much human time is required to replace the good or service and all resources used therein; more efficient and sustainable automation would drop the price of the product or service towards—even nearly equal to—zero.

An electronic currency might enable the reinterpretation of inflation and deflation at a fundamental and systemic level, by enabling the measurement of ratios of currencies in addition to sums of currencies. Prices and wages would not fluctuate with specific forms of inflation or deflation; instead, individual purchasing powers could fluctuate. In a monetary system measuring the total currency in circulation in real time, your personal cash balance can fluctuate directly in relation to events that otherwise would inflate or deflate prices and wages. Thus, value certifications reflecting real shifts in the balances of value across the economy can be simply, personally and immediately comprehended. Though you would remain intensely interested in fluctuations of your cash balance, you could rely upon stability in prices and wages no less than you can today.

In such a paradigm, an individual's purchasing power would change in relation to more genuine balances of service among human beings and Nature, not in relation to interests of arbitrage. As an electronic currency, time credits could contextualize the meaning, impact, and value of currency issuances or asset certifications (new capitalizations) by democracy. The impact to your purchasing power of any proposed Development Charter could be estimated roughly, instantly; your purchasing power may be projected to rise or fall based upon the proposed Charter; and your purchasing power can be indexed to the results actually measured in the future.

Dimensionalized metrics could also likely qualify permissions of time credits; sums of currency could be given "guidance systems" or "use parameters" or any other type of useful envelope.

One might ask why many of these innovations could not be fulfilled through electronic dollars. They might be. I do not yet have sufficient grasp of the factors to know for sure. My intuition tentatively suggests that a labor-time-denominated electronic currency could enable extraordinary tools for enhancing the fairness, transparency and perfection of economic activity.

Beyond the fundamentally important possibility of finding new ways to systemically reinterpret inflation (one of the principal reasons that notions of government-certified capitalizations and issues of currency have been rejected in the past), there are at least three other reasons to consider the potential utility of an alternatively-dimensioned electronic currency: (1) We must figure out a way to evolve our currency systems such that they are compatible with infinitely leveragable technologies that will profoundly alter the labor economy. (2) Any successor economic paradigm to canonical capitalism will, by obvious necessity, evolve alongside capitalism. It may turn out that the systematic structuring and operation of an emergent, parallel economy will require currency-level differentiation in order to self-govern and interface in a coherent manner with pre-existing economic activity. (3) If the programmatic objective of a more evolved economy is to enable each of us to measure how little we must use the currency, instead of measuring how much currency we have, then the labor-time-denominated currency may offer a simpler and truer construct with which to so align economic activity. Changing the dimensional meaning of our currency may help us program economics at its most fundamental level to be motivated by, among other qualities, how much liberty it can give human beings.

I will stress that either currency—dollar or a time credit—could likely function within the economic meta-system herein described. But either way, almost surely, our currency must become electronically measurable over time. It is hard to imagine how to reinterpret inflation and deflation if we cannot know, in nearly real time, at least the volume of currency in circulation. One possibility for gradually extending the utility of traditional currencies might be to use the serial numbers on bills to reference envelope information, perhaps enabling dollar sums and flows to be measured and indexed in new ways.

Realizing Maps and Frontiers

Enable economic activity intrinsically to realize and value true democracy and open science.

The economic paradigm presented above would, at least in principle of its intent, establish the framework within which to address the two problems I described in *Part I* concerning the maps and frontiers of capitalism: extension of economic models to account for and correct problematic animation by capital interests of democracy and all its limbs, and capitalism's inability to deal effectively with the emergence of transformative scientific knowledge.

To the first of these, the proposed paradigm is equipped with a motivation system that may reverse the invasion of democracy by capitalism. By (1) eliminating the traditional notion of the profit motive, (2) surfacing to transparent visibility information now hidden within P&Ls and confidentiality shelters, and (3) reducing over time, in the multitude of ways described above, the job preservation instinct that needlessly perpetuates what otherwise can be smaller, time-bound government programs, we may restore the truthfulness and genuineness of our democracy, and in the process perhaps achieve levels of efficiency and efficacy in its functioning that have never been seen before.

These changes to the motives of economic activity will make it far easier to reform the funding of our electoral systems.

To the second concern, the proposed economic paradigm is not only compatible with the introduction of scientific knowledge that may dramatically reduce the currency flows sustaining some existing industries, but thoroughly motivates the development of such knowledge and resulting technologies. The proposed model, again in principle of its intent, may permanently end our fears of economic depression brought about by deflationary overcapacity, and in the process, may liberate overcapacity to yield an elevated, efficient, and sustainable quality of life for every human being on Earth.

Chapter 7
A New Hope

"A non-violent revolution is not a program of seizure of power.
It is a program of transformation of relationships, ending in a
peaceful transfer of power."

-Mahatma Gandhi

It is a challenging and urgent matter to conceptualize a high-tech economic framework capable of ensuring collectively free and organically enriched individual human life—a system prepared to deal properly not only with globalization of trade, but with other possible transformations more epochal. I do not by any means claim to have identified the only answer, but I often wonder how many years we have left to conceive of a soft landing for civilization.

What is the sustainable model for an ideomechonomic system capable of supporting 6+ billion people on a single, fragile, blue-green Cosmic world? Surely Earth's 6+ billion sacred human beings must all be free to live fulfilled, free, healthy lives some day soon . . . for the alternative is too horrific to contemplate. One hopes that a critical number of brilliant economists and social theorists are busy at work outside the boxes of dogmatic assumptions, for it is no longer intellectually credible to argue that capitalism, in its neoliberal form, is the right model for third millennium society to implement as the foundation of Earth's ideomechonomic system.

In Evolving Economics, I present only a high-level overview of issues of profound complexity and subtlety. The proposed paradigm is by no means completely expressive of all considerations of relevance, and it is vital that

I stress the long-term nature of this vision. I ask the reader not to mistake the reach of this imagination as a naïve expectation of imminence. Rather I suggest understanding of the need for long term visions that can help provide compasses for short term direction of actions. Consider what has been said to represent a preliminary sketch, entirely subject to change through correction and better ideas. Don't let the isolatable defect or the inevitable question in my reasoning obscure other useful notions; let each idea stand or falls on its true merits. Look beyond the specifics of my sketch to the patterns it suggests, and feel free to use any of the notions I've offered here to inform your own alternative future vision of meta-systemic truth capable of enabling Nature's democracy of living beings to "aikido" the singularity we likely face.

But I believe that this egalibertarian compass is pointed in the right quadrant. I believe the kind of paradigm described can enable Nature-sustaining and human-respecting egalitarian and libertarian values to become intrinsic to ideomechonomic function. The solutions I propose are, in their essence, quite simple, as one would expect of proper basic corrections to the functioning of any system. Needless to say, their implications are unbelievably complex. That is an unavoidable consequence of the complexities and interdependencies in a vast ideomechonomic system. That fact does not mitigate possible suitability of proposed solutions to the problem set outlined in *Part I*. Indeed, diversity of implications of systemic change is a quality that must be offered by any model proposed as a means to evolve civilization towards sustainability within the timeframe we likely have to do so.

Our ingenuity has presented us with achingly huge questions, but there are equally powerful testimonies throughout the history books to guide our answers. One of the uniquely well-developed American convictions is that each human being, regardless of their sex, the color of their skin, the longitude and latitude of their birth, or the pattern of 1s and 0s in their financial accounts, is entitled to intrinsic rights and freedoms that may not be chained by a controlling regime. If we want such rights and freedoms to survive through the age in which the regime is defined, electronically governed, and motivated by high-tech global profit machines, it would seem logical that a shift is in order in the behaviors measured—and motivations enforced—by our monetary policies, valuation models, and financial statements. For unless we are willing to evolve our economic ideologies, while recognizing their vital strengths, we will become increasingly wounded and unwilling slaves to their existing kind of inhuman master; and we'll be increasingly aware of this condition too, as life's remote emotions are felt ever more clearly through high-fidelity media.

Regardless of whether my particular vision depicts the right kind of future for our economy, I believe we may soon glimpse new constraints and new possibilities within our systems of supply and demand. They will be driven by the need to resolve friction among human and environmental absolutes, increasingly arbitrary geopolitical borders, global ideomechonomic class divisions, the gift from science of near-zero-cost-of-supply energy, transportation, robotics and immersive communications, the threat of social self-destruction, and the demands of newly remembered, simple, compelling priorities and responsibilities in everyday human lives. The future civilization we seek to evolve must gift every human being the right to a natural life within an organic and stable biosphere, enjoying the freedoms won after millennia of intellectual and social evolution, after a century of horrifying war, responsibly employing the technology of modernity, and fulfilling the hopes of the honorable visionaries from every domain of human affairs.

Let us seek to envision, test, implement and participate in more evolved, egalitarian ideomechonomic systems, which can protect and restore life and serve us all sustainably. Let us consider how to evolve the aged yardsticks by which our economic machine measures its "growth" and "success", ever so carefully and fundamentally, so that the spiritless qualities of its robotic macrosystem can evolve to command less of the worship and time of our lives. It is possible for us to redefine the standards by which corporate equity symbols are calculated and tracked for "green" or "red". It is possible to envision networks of participant-controlled organizations in which we may freely choose to give and take as members, expanding our means of serving and enjoying each other. It is possible to seed-capitalize such organizations not through the ideology of taxation, but through a new ideology of democratic balancing of money supply in simple recognition of real future value and productivity. It is possible for our footprint to be dramatically lightened through new generations of wondrous technologies, never to be used destructively. It is possible for us to work together to reprogram and make newly transparent our vital, globalizing economic system, helping us avert self-extinction from impoverishment, resource cannibalism, cultural destruction and other terrors of ignorance.

Transformations of this order depend upon shifts in deeply-held attributions of value, and changes in values are not easy to make, because they are rooted in Darwinian depths of our consciousnesses. Such transformations represent shifts in hopes and changes in faiths.

At a time perhaps not too many years from now, many human beings will be able to look upon Earth from space with their own eyes, instead of through photographs and electronic screens. Viewed from orbit, the nighttime side of our world reveals a vast network of lights that mark the growth of human civilization. On the daylight side of our world, a staggeringly beautiful blue-green coral reef appears suspended in a starry ocean.

May we find the change of heart that we seek by asking ourselves what kind of world we want to live upon, down on that rare, precious, beautiful Cosmic shore below?

Endnotes

1   Smith, A. The Wealth of Nations, Book IV, Chapter I

2   Smith, A. Lectures on Justice, Policy, Revenue and Arms

3   Smith, A. Lecture in 1755, quoted by Dugald Stewart

4   The differences between profit and arbitrage have to do with risk and time in measures of "value", relevant in systems of capitalization that yield returns on the use of money. These differences are ethically significant to those who believe it is right that a money-sum have the abstract power to leverage itself to grow. To those who believe it is improper for a money-sum to have the abstract right to grow itself, the differences between profit and arbitrage are not ethically significant. 5 Greider, W. One World, Ready Or Not

6   Personal correspondence, September 30, 2001

7   Friedman, T. The Lexus and the Olive Tree, Anchor Books, 2000

8   Gomez, F. Financial Times Mastering Investment, June 11, 2001

9   Hayek, F.A. The Road to Serfdom, University of Chicago Press, 1944

10   Reported by AP from an interview in Focus newsmagazine, September 1, 2001

11   Hayek, F.A. The Road to Serfdom, University of Chicago Press, 1944

12   Personal correspondence, September 30, 2001

13   While such an assertion remains controversial amidst a noisy abundance of both good evidence and pseudoscience, no truth-respecting scholar of social or physical science should jump to the conclusion that the assertion is false without a thorough examination of the evidence, part of which is concisely explored in *UFOs and the National Security State*, Dolan, R., Keyhole Press, 2001.

14   If some pinnacle of political and capital interests is indeed aware of the plausibility of such technologies, it might make more understandable, though not necessarily more ethical or sensible, the Bush Administration's

attempts to expand profits from aging energy technologies before their obsolescence becomes publicly known, and also efforts to build military systems focused on new kinds of '21st century threats from rogue objects in the air and in space.'

[15] Wright, R. Nonzero, Vintage Books, 2001

[16] Hawken, Paul; Lovins, Amory; Lovins, Hunter L.: Natural Capitalism, Back Bay Books, 2001

[17] See *Book 1: Revolutions in Physics,* 2010

[18] Wright, R. Nonzero, Vintage Books, 2001

[19] Friedman, T. The Lexus and the Olive Tree, Anchor Books, 2000

[20] Gates, Jeff, The Ownership Solution, Addison Weseley, 1998

[21] Hawken, Paul; Lovins, Amory; Lovins, Hunter L.: Natural Capitalism, Back Bay Books, 2001

[22] Wilber, K., A Theory of Everything, Shambhala, 2000

[23] Factoring the costs of resource preservation and replacement into the prices of goods and services is an essential step towards a sustainable future. However, I do not believe that it is sufficient, for two reasons. First, increasing prices will reduce consumption, but it will not educate consumers. Second, increasing prices will exacerbate the quality of life divide between rich and poor people. We must properly price all goods and services to ensure sustainability, but we must also educate all people on the impacts of their consumption, and we must ensure that higher costs translate into shared access to resource-intensive infrastructure rather than further concentration of resource ownership in the hands of the wealthy few. Dimensionalized metrics educate consumers and can explicitly motivate shared access to rare resources.

[24] Essay received from Jeff Gates, 2001